A GARDENER'S GUIDE TO

CACTI
AND SUCCULENTS

How to grow these fascinating plants in the
home and greenhouse. Featuring 150 species

Gymnocalycium mihanovichii 'Hibotan'

Opuntia microdasys var. albispina

CACTI
AND SUCCULENTS

How to grow these fascinating plants in the
home and greenhouse. Featuring 150 species

PETER CHAPMAN
MARGARET MARTIN

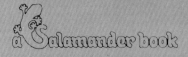

Published by Salamander Books Limited
LONDON

A Salamander Book

Published by Salamander Books Ltd.,
52 Bedford Row,
London WC1R 4LR.

© 1988 Salamander Books Ltd.

ISBN 0 86101 365 4

Distributed by
Hodder and Stoughton Services,
PO Box 6, Mill Road, Dunton Green,
Sevenoaks, Kent TN13 2XX.

All correspondence concerning the
content of this volume should be
addressed to Salamander Books Ltd.

Contents

Text and colour photographs are cross-referenced throughout as follows: 64 ▶ Silhouette drawings give an impression of a typical plant in a pot, not necessarily in scale with other plants.

The plants are arranged in alphabetical order of Latin name. Page numbers in **bold** refer to text entries; those in *italics* refer to photographs.

Credits

Authors: Peter Chapman and Margaret Martin are enthusiastic growers and collectors who have collaborated for over 20 years to photograph and write about cacti and other succulent plants. They have co-authored two books and contributed articles to countless other books and magazines. The advice they give in this book comes from first-hand experience.

Editor: Geoffrey Rogers
Designers: Barry Savage, Roger Hyde

Photographs: Many of the photographs have been taken by the authors. A full list of credits appears on page 160.
Principal line drawings: Maureen Holt.
© Salamander Books Ltd.
Silhouette scale drawings: Tyler/Camoccio Design Consultants
© Salamander Books Ltd.
Colour and monochrome reproductions: Bantam Litho Ltd., England.
Filmset: SX Composing Ltd., England.

Printed in Belgium by
Henri Proost & Cie, Turnhout.

Introduction

Although it is common practice to refer to 'Cacti and Succulent Plants', with one exception (the pereskias) all cacti are succulent to varying degrees and belong to one family, the Cactaceae, whereas succulents can belong to many different plant families. They all have in common the ability to store water in their tissues in order to survive periods of drought, and this makes them ideal plants for the busy or forgetful person; many can survive days or even weeks of dryness. Cacti in particular can be divided into desert and jungle types; the latter live on trees as epiphytes, often in association with orchids, in tropical rain forests. Epiphytes use trees for support only; they are not parasites. Such cacti are represented by the epiphyllums, rhipsalis species, the Christmas cactus, and similar plants.

Often any thick-leaved or spiny plant is called a cactus, sometimes incorrectly. The distinguishing feature is the 'areole', a small, pincushion-like structure arranged in numbers over the stems, from which any spines or hairs come. All cacti have areoles (and no other plants do), but they are not always easy to see. The cactus flower is also characteristic and is often large and beautiful. Many cacti bloom annually; but a few can never become large enough in an average amateur collection to do so. Cacti are 'stem succulents', that is, water is stored in greatly thickened stems and, apart from the exception mentioned earlier (the pereskias) and a few other rarities, they have no real leaves. Other succulents, coming as they do from many different families, have flowers as diverse as the families themselves. They have no areoles; any spines resemble rose thorns. Some African euphorbias are virtually leafless, and with their ribbed, thorny, succulent stems they closely resemble cacti.

Cacti come from the American continent and those found elsewhere in the world have been introduced at some time in the past. Many other succulents are native to Africa. Although mostly species plants are cultivated, some beautiful horticultural hybrids have been produced.

Naming and selection
Few of these plants have generally accepted common names, and their botanical names are prone to occasional change due to the latest fashionable scientific opinion. In this book we have used the most familiar names and given the recent alternative where applicable.

Situation and temperature
Almost all cacti and most other succulents can be overwintered at a temperature of 5°C (41°F) if kept dry, and cacti grown for flowers usually need this cold winter rest; indoors the window of an unheated room is the best place. Individual entries mention when a plant needs a rather higher winter temperature; greenhouse specimens can be brought indoors to save extra heating. Good light is essential for most succulents, and indoors the sunniest window should normally be used, remembering that the light is one-sided and the plants should be turned occasionally. In sunnier climes full sun in a greenhouse can cause scorch. The risk is reduced by good ventilation and few plants will scorch anywhere in the open air.

Potting mixtures and potting

Cacti and other succulent plants do not require an elaborate potting mixture; it really only needs to be well-drained. Either peat- or loam-based mixtures will do, but it is usually an advantage to mix in about one third of extra drainage material such as sharp sand or perlite, as the one thing all these plants dislike is any degree of waterlogging of the soil. Potting on – that is, transferring to a larger pot – is necessary when the plant has formed a mass of roots; it may or may not be necessary every year, depending on the rate of growth of the particular plant. Repotting can be carried out by shaking off as much of the old potting mixture as possible from the roots and replacing the plant in the same pot (thoroughly cleaned first) in fresh mixture. Spiny plants can be held in a fold of newspaper. The best time for this is early spring, at the beginning of the growing season; withhold watering for a few days afterwards to enable the roots to recover.

Watering and feeding

Most succulents grow in spring and summer when water can be freely given each time the potting mixture appears almost dry. In winter, any surplus water can easily cause rotting and complete dryness is normally necessary with greenhouse plants, but indoors an occasional watering may be needed to prevent undue shrivelling. (Any exceptions are mentioned in the text.) Many succulents, notably the freely flowering ones, benefit from a dose of fertilizer every two weeks during the spring and summer. A high-potassium type, such as is designed for tomatoes, should be used. But plants in soilless, peat-based potting mixtures, which contain no natural food, will need this throughout the growing season.

Propagation

Succulent plants can be raised from seed, which unless bought from a specialist nursery will probably be 'mixed'. Sow as for any greenhouse perennial at a temperature of 18-24°C (64-75°F). Be in no hurry to prick out; most seedlings can remain in the same pan for a year, unless very crowded. Keep them slightly moist and not too cold for their first winter. Plants that form offsets can be propagated by removing one or more, allowing them to dry for a few days to reduce the risk of rot, and then just pushing them into the usual potting mixture. This must be done in the full growing season, usually late spring or summer, when rooting should take place in a few weeks.

Pests

The main pest of these plants is the mealy bug, often seen as white cotton-wool patches and sometimes mistaken for a fungus. The pest itself hides within this, but sometimes appears, looking like a minute white woodlouse. Treatment with a proprietary spray will usually control these. But watch out for a more insidious relative, the root mealy bug, when you are repotting; minute white patches on the roots indicate this. Dip the infected roots in an insecticide before repotting and water occasionally with a similar material.

Right:
Acanthocalycium violaceum
*A most attractive globular cactus
beautifully spined and producing
splendid colourful blooms. It does
not become too large.* 17♦

Far right: **Agave filifera**
*Although a potential giant, this
succulent is slow-growing, and it
makes a very distinctive specimen
when small. The narrow leaves have
sharp spines at the tips.* 18♦

Below right: **Agave parviflora**
*This is one of the smaller agaves and
makes an attractive addition to any
collection. Offsets are usually
formed around the base. It is an easy
plant to raise from seed.* 18♦

Below:
Aeonium arboreum var. **nigrum**
*The almost black leaves of this
succulent make it a most unusual
plant. Good light is needed to keep
the leaves from becoming green.* 17♦

Above: **Agave victoria-reginae**
Probably the most beautiful of all the agaves, this slow-growing succulent does not usually form offsets, but is readily raised from seed. The attractive leaves are each tipped with a sharp spine. 19♦

Left: **Aloe jacunda**
This very attractive dwarf succulent soon produces offsets from the base to form a group, and is free-flowering. Its need for partial shade makes it ideal as a room plant, for a not too sunny window. 20♦

Above right: **Aloe variegata**
The very well-known Partridge Breast Aloe is ideally suited to the living-room as it thrives in shade. Pink flowers are sometimes produced at the end of a long stem. Very little water is needed. 21♦

Right: **Ancistrocactus scheeri**
A slow-growing cactus with very beautiful spines and flowers. As it has a thick, fleshy root, it is prone to rotting and needs very careful watering. Offsets are not usually produced. 22♦

Left: Aporocactus flagelliformis
The popular Rat's Tail Cactus, with its long hanging stems and colourful flowers, is a 'must' for a basket – really the only way to grow it. 23♦

Right: Ariocarpus fissuratus
Looking more like a chunk of stone than a cactus, this plant can in fact produce a most beautiful flower. It is very slow-growing. 24♦

Below right: Astrophytum asterias
Another unusual cactus, entirely without spines, but producing most attractive yellow flowers. Well worth the extra care it needs. 25♦

Below: Aporocactus mallisonii
Another ideal subject for a hanging basket, this cactus – which is actually a hybrid – has masses of trailing stems and large flowers. 23♦

Left: Astrophytum myriostigma
A simple astrophytum to cultivate and also easy to handle, being quite spineless. The silvery hairy scales give it a rock-like appearance. 26♦

Below: **Astrophytum ornatum**
A spiny astrophytum, which needs to be fairly large before flowering but is nevertheless an interesting addition to any collection. 26♦

Bottom: **Borzicactus aureispinus**
This somewhat unusual cactus needs careful positioning to allow for the beautiful long stems with their golden spines. 27♦

Left: Carpobrotus edulis
This succulent can be grown out of doors in mild regions of temperate countries, ideally in a sunny rock garden, where its sprawling stems and colourful flowers are a delight. Edible fruits are produced. 29♦

Below: Cephalocereus senilis
'Old Man Cactus' aptly describes this plant, with its mass of twisted white hairs and almost no spines. Although large in nature, it makes an ideal pot specimen. 29♦

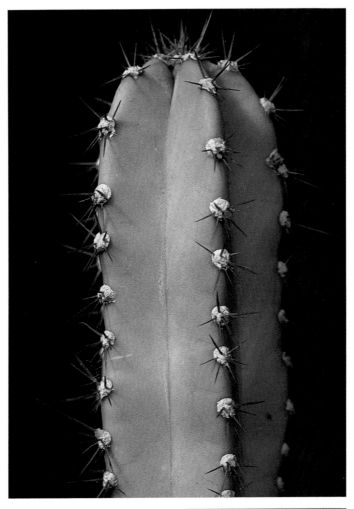

Above: **Cereus peruvianus**
Although it can be a giant in the wild, the attractively spined, slender stems of this cactus make an ideal contrast with the more globular plants in the collection. It is grown for its shape and form rather than its flowers, which are not produced by small specimens. 30◗

Right: **Ceropegia woodii**
This succulent, with its long trailing stems, needs to be grown on a plastic trellis or similar support, where it can show off its curious but most attractive flowers and small fleshy leaves to the best advantage. Otherwise, let the stems trail over the edge of the pot. 30◗

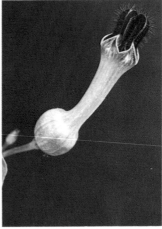

Acanthocalycium violaceum
- **Full sun**
- **Temp: 5-30°C (41-86°F)**
- **Water with care**

Acanthocalycium violaceum is a cylindrical plant about 12cm (4.7in) in diameter. During summer, it produces large numbers of beautiful violet flowers, about 5cm (2in) across. Even during winter the plant is attractive, and the stout yellow spines show up well against the dark green of the stem. This cactus does not offset easily, certainly not as a young plant; many apparently solitary plants do occasionally form offsets with age.

A good potting mixture is two parts of loam- or peat-based material to one part of sharp sand or perlite. *A. violaceum* should be watered with caution even during the summer growing period. Always allow it to dry out between waterings and if possible water on a sunny day. Feed every two weeks with a high-potassium (tomato) fertilizer when the buds form. If it should lose its roots, allow the plant to dry for two or three days and repot in fresh, well-drained mixture. Keep in a well-lit position.

Take care
Water sparingly. 8♦

Aeonium arboreum 'Nigrum' ('Zwartkop')
- **Full sun**
- **Temp: 5-30°C (41-86°F)**
- **Water occasionally in winter**

An attractive, robust succulent with almost black glossy leaves arranged in a rosette that can be as much as 20cm (8in) across. The stem carrying it is about 1.5cm (0.6in) thick and as it gradually elongates one is left with a rosette of leaves on about 30cm (12in) of bare stem, any lower leaves having fallen off. Cut off the leafy top with a short piece of the stem, let it dry for a couple of days and then just push it into the surface of fresh potting mixture. It will soon rot to form a flat, compact plant once more. Keep the old stem; it will send out many small rosettes, which in their turn can be removed and rooted.

This aeonium makes a good houseplant but needs plenty of light or the leaves will tend to lose their beautiful dark colour and turn greenish. Although it will withstand a lower temperature, it does not need it and will thrive in a normal living-room. Use any good standard potting mixture.

Take care
Mealy bugs like to live between the leaves. 8♦

Agave filifera
- **Full sun**
- **Temp: 5-30°C (41-86°F)**
- **Water with care**

Agave filifera forms a rosette 65cm (26in) across; each leathery leaf is 3cm (1.2in) wide and ends in a stout spine. The leaves are dark green in colour with white threads along the edge. This agave will eventually throw up a flower stem 2.5m (8ft) high, on the end of which are purple and green bell-like flowers. The main rosette dies after flowering, but new rosettes will form at the base of the old plant. The lifespan of the main rosette is 8-25 years.

Because of its tough leaves, *A. filifera* is very resistant to a dry atmosphere. If it is kept indoors during the winter months, place it outdoors during the summer. It needs sun during the growing period to keep it a good colour and shape. It is ideal for a patio or veranda.

This agave will grow in any loam- or peat-based medium. Water generously during very hot weather but keep only slightly moist during winter or periods of cloudy, damp weather.

Agave parviflora
- **Full sun**
- **Temp: 5-30°C (41-86°F)**
- **Do not overwater**

One of the smallest of the agaves, *Agave parviflora* is ideal for a small greenhouse. The adult rosette is 18cm (7in) across, and the slender dark green leaves have white edges and white marginal threads. Eventually the plant will flower and die. The flower stem is about 1m (39in) high and carries pale yellow flowers. The agave will probably be over five years old when it flowers, and young plantlets will form around the dying rosette. These should be removed and potted up. Because of its attractive form, *A. parviflora* makes a good houseplant. When warm weather comes, put the plant outdoors in full sun; this will keep it in good health.

A good loam- or peat-based medium will suit this plant. It should be repotted annually. During hot weather, water freely: but keep it just moist during the winter and wet, cloudy weather. Agaves, with their tough leaves, present a problem to any insect pests.

Take care
Beware of the stout spines. 9♦

Take care
Repot each year. 9♦

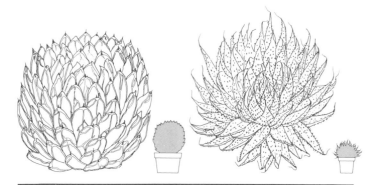

Agave victoria-reginae
- Full sun
- Temp: 5-30°C (41-86°F)
- Water with care

Agave victoria-reginae is the most beautiful of the small agaves. It is a densely leaved rosette: the leaves are 15cm (6in) long, dark green in colour with beautiful white markings. Each leaf ends in a terminal spine, which should be treated with respect. *A. victoria-reginae* can withstand a very dry atmosphere and may be used as a houseplant during the winter months, but in the summer growing period it needs full sun to bring out its beautiful colouring.

Like all agaves, this species has a long flower stem, 3-4m (10-13ft) in height. The flowers are cream. After flowering the rosette dies, and unfortunately there are unlikely to be any offsets. But you may well have had the plant for 10 years before it flowers.

Any good loam- or peat-based potting mixture is suitable for this plant. It should be repotted annually. The plant may be watered freely during hot sunny weather but should be kept fairly dry at other times.

Take care
Avoid the sharp spines. 10♦

Aloe aristata
- Partial shade
- Temp: 5-30°C (41-86°F)
- Water occasionally in winter

Although some aloes are impossible giants, this one is ideal for a greenhouse or windowsill collection. It forms tough green rosettes about 10-15cm (4-6in) across; clumps of up to 12 rosettes may eventually be produced. But this is no problem, because individual rosettes can easily be detached and grown as new plants. Narrow leaves within the rosette are 8-10cm (3.2-4in) long with slightly raised white spots. Small greenish flowers are produced in a cluster on the end of thin stems up to 50cm (20in) high.

Preference for partial shade makes this and other aloes ideal houseplants, but do not put them in any dark corner; merely avoid full summer sunlight. If kept in a living-room give some water in winter, but in a colder greenhouse this succulent is best allowed to be almost dry; only water if it shrivels. *A. aristata* is easy to grow in any good potting mixture, and extra drainage material is not necessary.

Take care
Divide the plant before it becomes too large.

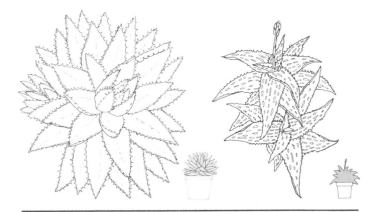

Aloe brevifolia
- **Partial shade**
- **Temp: 5-30°C (41-86°F)**
- **Keep slightly moist in winter**

Although this succulent can make a large clump of 12 or more heads, the individual plants are only up to 8cm (3.2in) across, and these can easily be separated before the plant becomes unmanageable. So it is one of the easiest plants to propagate. Each head consists of about 30 fleshy leaves, up to 6cm (2.4in) long and 2cm (0.8in) broad at the base. Upper surfaces are smooth and the few soft spines are confined to the undersides; the edges are furnished with blunt white teeth. A flower stem of about 30cm (12in), with small scarlet tubular flowers at the end, enhances the beauty of this plant, which is very easy to grow. Its need for some shade from summer sun and its wide temperature tolerance make it an ideal houseplant. It is also tolerant with regard to its soil requirements; any good standard potting mixture, either loam- or peat-based, will be quite satisfactory. Water this aloe quite freely in spring and summer, and give enough in winter to prevent shrivelling.

Take care
Avoid dark corners indoors.

Aloe jacunda
- **Partial shade**
- **Temp: 5-30°C (41-86°F)**
- **Keep slightly moist in winter**

A true dwarf succulent plant, this is one of the most attractive of the aloes. It consists of prettily mottled fleshy leaves, forming a compact rosette 8-9cm (3.2-3.5in) across. Individual leaves are up to 4cm (1.6in) long and 2cm (0.8in) broad at the base. This delightful little aloe branches freely from the base and soon forms an attractive clump. Excess heads can easily be removed, complete with roots, for propagation. Typical small, tubular aloe flowers, rose-pink in colour, are produced on stems up to 30cm (12in) long.

Any good potting mixture is normally well enough drained for this aloe. Grow it indoors by all means, keeping it in a light window, but avoid full sun. It can even be planted out in the garden during spring and summer. It should be watered freely in spring and summer. Indoors in winter it will need more water than in a greenhouse.

Take care
Watch out for slugs on plants in the garden. 10♦

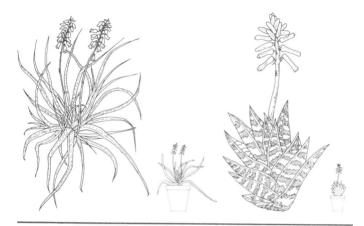

Aloe x 'Sabra'
- **Partial shade**
- **Temp: 5-28°C (41-83°F)**
- **Water occasionally during winter flowering**

This hybrid aloe was produced by an English nurseryman and named in honour of his daughter. It is a very pretty, relatively small-growing succulent with long, narrow, finely toothed, purplish-green leaves dappled with white. Individual leaves grow up to 20cm (8in) long, but are only about 12mm (0.5in) wide at the base. The plant forms offsets freely, eventually producing a clump of heads, each of which can give rise to a flower stem up to 20cm (8in) long, tipped with about 30 pinkish-white blooms, opening in succession from the top. A clump about 13cm (5in) across would probably consist of five to eight heads.

This aloe flowers in the winter and it is essential to give the plant some water at this time, with a short, almost dry, resting period after flowering, until early spring. During the rest of the year it may be watered freely. A good, well-drained potting mixture is needed; add about one third of sharp sand or perlite to a standard mix.

Take care
Full summer sun can cause the leaf tips to dry out.

Aloe variegata
(Partridge breast aloe)
- **Partial shade**
- **Temp: 10-30°C (50-86°F)**
- **Keep dry in winter**

This is certainly one of the best-known succulent plants. It thrives on many windowsills in homes and offices, and its success indicates the chief cultivation tip – it is better as a houseplant than in a greenhouse environment. The surprising thing is how little water the plant seems to need, even indoors. The leaves have a thickened 'V' section and are up to 15cm (6in) long in mature plants, though most specimens are much smaller. They are bright green, marbled with whitish bands. Although so common, this is a delightful plant, enhanced occasionally by the appearance of bright pink, tubular flowers on a stem up to 30cm (12in) long.

Although this aloe seems to thrive on neglect, it is possible to go too far in this respect, witness the miserable, dried-up specimens sometimes seen! Add about one third extra sharp sand or perlite to any good potting mixture, either loam- or peat-based.

Take care
Water only in spring and summer when almost dried out. 11♦

Aloinopsis schooneesii

- **Full sun**
- **Temp: 5-30°C (41-86°F)**
- **Keep dry in winter**

Aloinopsis schooneesii is often listed in catalogues under its older name of *Nananthus schooneesii*. This little South African plant is a leafy succulent; each head has about 10 fleshy blue-green leaves. The plant clusters, but may be kept for several years in a 7.5cm (3in) pot. It must be placed in a sunny position if it is to flower well.

The golden-yellow flowers are produced continuously through the summer months. Each flower lasts for several days. The flowers are about 1.5cm (0.6in) across.

This succulent needs a very open soil; half loam-based mixture and half sharp sand or perlite is suitable. It is not necessary to repot annually; it is better to break the cluster up every three or four years in the spring. Pull the heads off, dry for two days and then pot up.

Water the plant freely during summer, allowing to dry between waterings.

Take care
Do not water during winter.

Ancistrocactus scheeri

- **Full sun**
- **Temp: 5-30°C (41-86°F)**
- **Keep dry in winter**

A beautifully spined, very attractive cactus that is well worth the little extra attention needed to cultivate it. The roughly spherical stem, which does not normally form offsets, carries strong yellowish spines, sometimes as long as 4cm (1.6in). A good specimen is around 7cm (2.8in) across. The funnel-shaped flowers, yellowish-green in colour, are about 2.5cm (1in) wide.

Admittedly, this is not one of the easiest of cacti to grow, but it should thrive if its requirements are understood. The main difficulty is that it has large, fleshy roots that have a tendency to disappear at the slightest amount of excess water, and for this reason some specimens are grown grafted. But all should be well if you use a very open potting mixture, made by using equal parts of sharp sand or perlite and a standard loam- or peat-based mix; water only in spring and summer.

Take care
If roots are lost, cut to clean tissue, dry and repot. 11♦

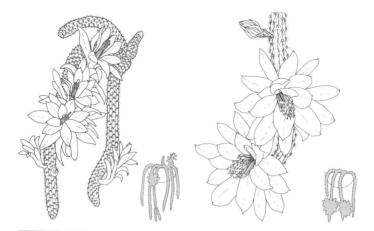

Aporocactus flagelliformis

(Rat's-tail cactus)
- **Diffuse sunlight**
- **Temp: 5-30°C (41-86°F)**
- **Keep moist all year**

A beautiful plant for a hanging basket, this cactus will grow happily in a window. The long slender stems may reach a length of 2m (6.5ft); they are closely ribbed and densely covered with small brown spines. In early spring, the stems are covered with vivid cerise flowers; these are tubular, 5cm (2in) long, and last for several days.

A loam- or peat-based mixture is suitable for this plant. Feed with a liquid tomato fertilizer once every two weeks during the growing period. Repot annually. Never allow the plant to become completely dry, even in winter. In summer, water generously.

When the plant becomes too large, one of the tails may be cut off, dried for two days and potted up. Early summer is the best time for rooting cuttings. Mealy bug can be a serious pest. It is easy to overlook them on a large plant. Treat the plant with a systemic insecticide.

Take care
Never let this plant dry out. 12♦

Aporocactus mallisonii

- **Diffuse sunlight**
- **Temp: 5-30°C (41-86°F)**
- **Keep damp all year**

An excellent plant for a hanging basket, this cactus will thrive in a warm living-room but does need plenty of light. The stout stems reach a length of about 1m (39in); they are deeply ribbed and covered in short spines. In early summer, large numbers of brilliant red flowers are carried along the stems.

A good loam- or peat-based mixture is needed. Repot annually. During the summer growing period, water generously and use a liquid tomato fertilizer every two weeks.

A. mallisonii (now known as x *Heliaporus smithii*) is a hybrid and can only be propagated vegetatively. When the plant has outgrown its accommodation, cut off one of the stems. Dry for two days and pot up. Propagation is most successful in early summer. Mealy bug is the chief pest that attacks this cactus. Inspect the stems regularly. Spray with a proprietary insecticide if an infestation is found.

Take care
Never let this plant dry out. 12♦

Argyroderma octophyllum

- Full sun
- Temp: 5-30°C (41-86°F)
- Keep dry in winter

This is a stemless plant with one pair of fat, egg-shaped leaves, which are blue-green in colour. This plant will never grow more than 3cm (1.2in) long, and is ideal for a small, sunny greenhouse. The yellow flowers appear from the cleft between the leaves in late summer. The flowers are about 2cm (0.8in) across and open on sunny afternoons, closing in the evening. The flowers last for several days.

During spring, the old pair of leaves will start to shrivel and a new plant will emerge from between them. No water should be given until the old leaves have completely dried up. Continue watering on sunny days until the autumn. Keep dry through the winter.

Grow in a mixture of half loam-based medium and half sharp sand or perlite. Repot every three or four years. Mealy bug and root mealy bug can be serious pests; water with a proprietary insecticide.

Take care
Never overwater, or the plant will become bloated.

Ariocarpus fissuratus var. lloydii
(Living rock)

- Full sun
- Temp: 5-30°C (41-86°F)
- Always water carefully

Ariocarpuses are among the rarest and most interesting of the cacti but are suitable only for greenhouse cultivation. These plants grow in desert conditions in the blazing sun. For successful cultivation they need the maximum sunlight, a very open mixture (half loam-based medium, half sharp sand or perlite) and careful watering. Water on sunny days in summer, and keep dry in winter.

A. fissuratus bears a close resemblance to a chunk of rock. It has a thickened taproot crowned by large flattened tubercles. The tubercles are greyish in colour with creamy wool among the new growth. The large satiny pink flowers appear from the centre of the plant. They open in late autumn or early winter. A mature specimen is 15cm (6in) across, and may have taken 20 years to reach that size. Mealy bug may attack the new, tender growth. Inspect the woolly centre of the plant for signs of these pests. If found, treat with a suitable insecticide.

Take care
Never overwater. 13♦

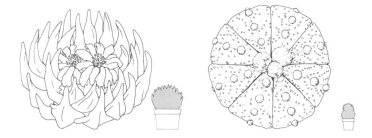

Ariocarpus trigonus
- Full sun
- Temp: 5-30°C (41-86°F)
- Water very carefully

Astrophytum asterias
- Full sun
- Temp: 5-30°C (41-86°F)
- Do not overwater

Ariocarpus trigonus is a rare and unusual cactus. The plant has long upright tubercles arranged like a crown on the large taproot. Most specimens seen in cultivation are not more than 13cm (5in) across. The tubercles are brownish-grey in colour. The flowers are produced from the centre of the plant in late autumn or early winter. They are pale yellow with a satiny sheen.

Water with the greatest care, on sunny days only, so that any surplus moisture dries up quickly. Keep dry in the winter. The soil must be very well drained: a loam-based mixture to which an equal volume of sharp sand or perlite has been aded is suitable. Although slow-growing, ariocarpuses can swell at the neck of the plant just below soil level and jam themselves in their pots. Make sure there is a space of about 1cm (0.4in) between the plant and the rim of the pot. Because of its need for strong light, *A. trigonus* needs greenhouse cultivation.

Take care
Do not let soil get compacted.

Astrophytum asterias looks like a grey-green sea urchin; it could never be confused with any other cactus. Eventually it forms a flattened hemisphere about 10cm (4in) across. The stem is made up of eight spineless ribs, and the skin is covered with white spots. These vary from plant to plant: some specimens are beautifully covered in white polka dots, whereas others may have very few markings. The flowers open continuously through the summer; they are pale shiny yellow with a red throat, and sweetly scented. Seedlings about 2.5cm (1in) across will flower.

Never overwater and keep the soil completely dry during winter. A very open soil, half loam- or peat-based mixture and half sharp sand or perlite, is suitable. To ensure continuous flowering, keep the plant in the sunniest part of the greenhouse and feed every two weeks with a tomato fertilizer when the buds form.

Take care
Avoid watering on dull days. 13♦

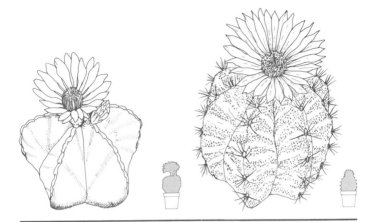

Astrophytum myriostigma
(Bishop's mitre)
- **Full sun**
- **Temp: 5-30°C (41-86°F)**
- **Dry winter rest**

Astrophytum myriostigma is a cylindrical plant eventually reaching a diameter of 20cm (8in). The dark green skin is completely covered with silvery scales. The number of ribs varies from four to eight. They are spineless, but the prominent areoles give the plant the appearance of having been buttoned into its skin. The flowers appear on the top of the plant continuously throughout the summer. They are yellow with a reddish throat and a sweet scent.

This is the easiest of the astrophytums to grow. A loam-based or peat-based mixture plus one third extra grit is suitable. Water freely throughout the summer, giving a liquid tomato fertilizer every two weeks, but keep dry in winter. This cactus is a native of the Mexican deserts and in cultivation needs the maximum light available. Mealy bug and root mealy bug can be a nuisance. Small white mealy bugs look very much like white scales.

Take care
Allow to dry between waterings. 14♦

Astrophytum ornatum
- **Full sun**
- **Temp: 5-30°C (41-86°F)**
- **Water with care**

Astrophytum ornatum does not bloom until it is about 15cm (6in) high, and it will probably take about 10 years to reach flowering size. But even without flowers, this is an attractive cactus. The stem is divided by eight ribs, which carry stout amber-coloured spines. The dark green skin has bands of silvery scales running across it. The pale yellow flowers are carried on top of the plant and are sweetly scented.

To keep the vivid colouring of this cactus, it needs sun. A useful mix is two parts loam- or peat-based medium plus one part sharp sand or perlite. Water generously throughout the summer, allowing to dry out before watering again. When the buds form give a dose of tomato fertilizer every two weeks. Keep the soil dry throughout the winter. Repot the plant annually, and inspect the roots for any grey ashy deposits, a sign that root mealy bug is present; if it is, water with an insecticide.

Take care
Make sure drips in the greenhouse do not spoil winter dryness. 14♦

Borzicactus (Matucana) aureiflora

- Full sun
- Temp: 5-30°C (41-86°F)
- Keep dry in winter

The two names given for this cactus indicate that it also has been subjected to re-classification and it is more likely that you will meet it under *Matucana.* Although in nature the globular stem can reach a diameter of 30cm (12in), specimens in cultivation are likely to be much smaller, with a flattened rather than a globular stem. A number of blunt ribs carry colourful, stout spreading spines. Bright yellow flowers, usually about 3cm (1.2in) across, are formed at the top of the stem in summer.

Use a porous potting mixture, which you can make by adding about one third of sharp sand or perlite to a standard loam- or peat-based material. Water this cactus quite freely in summer and feed once every two weeks or so with a high-potassium fertilizer, such as is given to tomatoes. Really good light will help to develop the fine spine coloration; give it full sunlight if at all possible.

Take care
If in a room, put it in the sunniest window.

Borzicactus aureispinus

- Full sun
- Temp: 5-30°C (41-86°F)
- Keep dry in winter

The long elegant stems of this unusual cactus make it a fascinating addition to any collection. *Borzicactus* was previously called *Hildewintera aureispina* and *Winterocereus aureispinus,* being a victim to the name changes that take place all too frequently among cacti (and other plants!). With stems up to 50cm (20in) long and 4-5cm (1.6-2.0in) wide, it is somewhat of a challenge to manage. Branches come freely from the base, so that a cluster of stems is eventually formed. Either tie them to a stout cane pushed into the pot or use a half-pot, letting the stems trail over the edge and along the greenhouse staging or a shelf. The stems glisten with bright golden spines, and beautiful salmon-pink flowers can be expected on older specimens.

Grow borzicactus in a good standard loam- or peat-based potting mixture, to which has been added a third sharp sand or perlite.

Take care
Mealy bugs can hide among the dense spines. 14♦

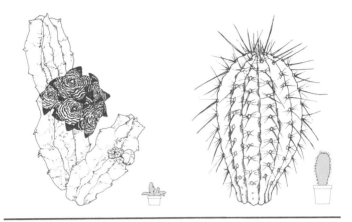

Caralluma europaea
- **Full sun**
- **Temp: 10-30°C (50-86°F)**
- **Keep moderately dry in winter**

A delightful little succulent plant which, although related to the 'carrion' flowers, has nothing unpleasant about it. The four-angled, slightly toothed stems (no spines) branch freely and reach a length of about 10cm (4in). The plant has a somewhat creeping habit. Star-shaped yellow flowers with deep purple markings, 2cm (0.8in) across, are produced in summer.

Caralluma europaea is an easy plant to cultivate, the only likely trouble being winter care. Although it will survive lower temperatures than the suggested 10°C (50°F), it may succumb to fungus attack (usually indicated by black marks on the stems) unless completely dry, when it is likely to shrivel badly. So keep it warmer, indoors if necessary, and give enough water in winter to prevent shrivelling. With a good, well-drained potting mixture (one part sharp sand or perlite to two parts of a standard mix) you can water it freely in summer.

Take care
Avoid cold and damp conditions.

Carnegia gigantea
(Saguaro)
- **Full sun**
- **Temp: 5-30°C (41-86°F)**
- **Keep dry in winter**

Symbolic of many Western films and also used as the state sign of Arizona, this is one of the largest cacti, but because it is very slow-growing it is quite suitable as a pot plant. Although in nature it can reach a height of 15m (50ft), it takes about 200 years to do so; hardly likely to embarrass the collector! An average domestic specimen would be about 15cm (6in) high in ten years. It forms a green, ribbed column with short spines, and will not produce the up-pointing arms characteristic of giant desert plants; it is unlikely to flower in the owner's lifetime. Although not particularly spectacular as a potted cactus, it is nevertheless of interest because of its association with the desert giants.

Grow *C. gigantea* in a particularly well-drained potting mixture; add one part of sharp sand or perlite to two parts of a good standard loam- or peat-based material. A top dressing of gravel 1cm (0.4in) thick will help to avoid rotting at the base.

Take care
Never overwater this cactus.

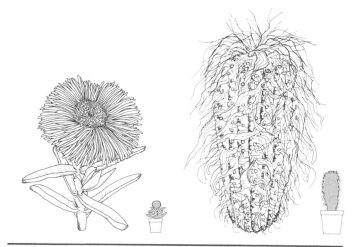

Carpobrotus edulis
(Hottentot fig)
- **Full sun**
- **Frost-free conditions**
- **Water generously in hot weather**

Like many shrubby succulents, *C. edulis* does better if planted outdoors during warm weather. It can either be lifted in the autumn, or cuttings can be taken in late summer and wintered indoors. In mild regions it can remain outside.

The plant is a strongly growing shrub with prostrate branches 1m (39in) long. It can be grown against a small wall and the branches allowed to trail over it. The large triangular leaves are grass-green in colour. Although this is not a prolific flowerer, the blooms are large, about 10cm (4in) across, and a vivid magenta, yellow or orange in colour.

If grown outdoors the plant will suffer from the same pests as other garden plants, and should be given similar treatment. It should be placed in a sunny position and given an occasional watering during prolonged dry weather. Cuttings should be wintered on a light windowsill or in a frost-free greenhouse. Keep slightly moist.

Take care
Restart when it becomes untidy. 15♦

Cephalocereus senilis
(Old man cactus)
- **Full sun**
- **Temp: 7-30°C (45-86°F)**
- **Water very carefully**

In its native Mexico, this cactus forms a column 12m (40ft) high and 45cm (18in) across. These plants are said to be 200 years old, so there is little fear of a seedling outgrowing its accommodation. The white flowers are not produced until the plant is 6m (20ft) high, so this cactus must be grown for the beauty of its form.

The pale green stem with its yellow spines is completely hidden by long, white hairs. These will pick up dust, so to keep the plant gleaming white, shampoo it with a dilute detergent solution and rinse thoroughly; choose a hot sunny day. With advancing age, the lower hairs will inevitably become permanently discoloured. The upper part of the stem may be cut, dried for three days, and potted up. Take cuttings in late spring.

A very open soil – half loam-based mixture and half grit – and a dry winter rest are essential. Keep this cactus in the warmest, sunniest position available.

Take care
Avoid cold, damp conditions. 15♦

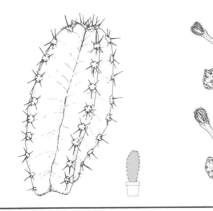

Cereus peruvianus
- **Full sun**
- **Temp: 5-30°C (41-86°F)**
- **Water generously in summer**

Ceropegia woodii
- **Full sun**
- **Temp: 7-30°C (45-86°F)**
- **Keep slightly moist in winter**

This columnar plant forms a handsome addition to any cactus collection. It is a vigorous plant and in a matter of a few years will form a blue-green column about 2m (6.5ft) high. The stem is ribbed, and the ribs carry stout spines. It is possible to flower this cereus in cultivation; the large white flowers open at night. In the wild, this plant will reach a height of 9m (30ft). When it reaches the roof of the greenhouse, cut the cereus about 1m (39in) from the top, dry for three days, and then pot up the top. The base will send out branches, which can be used for propagation.

   Grow in a loam-based mixture and repot annually. Water generously during summer, and feed about once a month with a liquid fertilizer with a high potassium content (tomato fertilizer). Keep dry in winter. *C. peruvianus* is tough and vigorous, and unlikely to be bothered by pests.

Take care
Do not allow this plant to become potbound. 16♦

This plant has small heart-shaped leaves on long wiry stems. If the plant is kept moist, the leaves are thin and green; but if it is kept dry, the leaves thicken and attractive silvery markings develop. *C. woodii* makes a pretty plant for a hanging basket. But it looks even better if the stems are coiled around the top of a pan. Then the flowers stand up from the stems like tiny purple candles. The stems will root into the soil and form small tubers. After flowering, horn-shaped seed pods may develop. Inside the pod are flat seeds, each attached to its own tiny parachute.

   A rich but porous soil and a sunny position are needed. Water fairly generously in summer, but keep just slightly moist in winter. *C. woodii* forms small tubers but the actual root system is shallow, so grow it in a pan or a half-pot. If seeds set on the plant, sow the seed as soon as released and small seedlings should come up quickly.

Take care
Avoid winter cold and dampness. 16♦

Chamaecereus silvestrii
(Peanut cactus)
- **Full sun**
- **Temp: 0-30°C (32-86°F)**
- **Keep dry in winter**

Sometimes recently listed as *Lobivia silvestrii* (another victim of botanical name changes), it seems more appropriate here to use the name of so many years standing. The spreading stems are somewhat finger-like in shape and size, bright green in colour and covered with short spines. Offsets, somewhat resembling green peanuts, appear along the length of the stems, hence the popular name. They detach themselves at the slightest touch, and can be potted up at once – surely the easiest cactus to propagate! But the great joy of this plant is the brilliant scarlet flowers, 4cm (1.6in) across; produced in profusion, they almost cover the stems during spring and summer.

This is not a fussy plant, so grow it in any good potting mixture. Water freely in spring and summer. One of the hardiest cacti, it will survive in a cold frame if quite dry.

Take care
Keep cold in winter to encourage good flowering. 33♦

Chamaecereus silvestrii, orange hybrid
- **Full sun**
- **Temp: 0-30°C (32-86°F)**
- **Keep dry in winter**

Taking advantage of the close relationship between *Chamaecereus* and *Lobivia*, plant breeders have produced hybrids between these two groups of cacti. The result is a compact plant with short, stubby, upright, branching stems. Offsets are still formed and do not fall off so readily as with *C. silvestrii* itself, but propagation by means of these is still very easy. Flowers, in this case bright orange and about 4cm (1.6in) in diameter, are freely produced in spring and summer. Other similar hybrids exist with red and also yellow blooms.

Water this cactus freely in spring and summer and feed every two weeks with a high-potassium fertilizer, from when the buds form. This will encourage flowering, as will a cold winter rest; use an unheated room in the house. Grow in a good standard loam- or peat-based potting mixture. Extra grit is needed only if there is doubt about drainage.

Take care
Watch for mealy bugs. 33♦

Cleistocactus straussii

(Silver torch)
- **Full sun**
- **Temp: 5-30°C (41-86°F)**
- **Water generously in summer**

Cleistocactus straussii is a slender column that will reach a height of 2m (6.5ft); the stem branches from the base. The plant is densely covered in short white spines, which give the plant a silvery gleam in the sunlight. Mature specimens flower freely in cultivation. The carmine flowers are carried on the sides of the columns and have a very characteristic shape: they consist of a long narrow tube with an opening only large enough for the stamens to protrude.

This is a vigorous cactus and to keep healthy it needs a good loam-based mixture and an annual repotting. Water generously during summer, give an occasional high-potassium liquid feed, and keep it dry in winter. To encourage flowering, put it in the sunniest position available. Some of the stems may be removed and used as cuttings if the plant is becoming too crowded.

Take care
Do not let this cactus become potbound. 34♦

Conophytum bilobum
- **Full sun**
- **Temp: 5-30°C (41-86°F)**
- **Give completely dry rest**

Conophytums are ideal plants for the small greenhouse but they need full sun. *C. bilobum* is one of the easiest species to grow. The two stemless leaves are fused to form a heart-shaped plant body, which is smooth and pale green in colour. The shining yellow flowers appear from the cleft between the leaves in late summer.

When to water can be a problem. Conophytums grow in late summer and autumn; but conditions in the greenhouse and the climatic conditions outside can influence growth, and watering is best based on observation. When watering stops, the plant body will slowly shrivel. Eventually two or three new heads emerge from the old plant. When the previous year's growth has shrivelled to a paper-thin skin, regular watering can start. It is advisable to give conophytums one good soaking in spring. Pot in very open mixture.

Take care
Make sure the winter dryness is not spoilt by drips in the greenhouse. 34♦

Top: **Chamaecereus silvestrii**
*The Peanut Cactus is very popular
and easy to grow. Finger-like stems
are covered with brilliant flowers in
spring and summer.* 31♦

Above:
Chamaecereus yellow hybrid
*One of the many attractive hybrids of
this cactus. A more compact plant
than the top one.* 31♦

Far left: Cleistocactus strausii
This beautiful silvery column can reach a height of over 100cm (39in) but is unlikely to out-grow its welcome in the average collection. Branches usually form at the base; small flowers are produced on older plants but do not open fully. 32♦

Left: Conophytum frutescens
Possibly the most attractive of a delightful group of miniature succulents. The plant consists of two very fleshy leaves to each head, from between which the flower grows. 49♦

Below left: Conophytum bilobum
This conophytum, one of the 'stemless mesembs', readily forms compact little clumps with masses of quite large yellow flowers. A most interesting collection can be made of conophytums alone, as they are all beautiful and take up very little space. 32♦

Below: Copiapoa cinerea
Flowers are not readily produced on these little cacti in temperate climates, but their compact growth and the attractive contrast between plant and spine colour make them nevertheless well worth growing. 49♦

Far left: Coryphantha vivipara
A free-flowering small cactus, which usually forms a clump of globular stems. With a good, well-drained soil it can survive low temperatures. 50♦

Top left: Crassula deceptrix
This miniature succulent has a mass of branched stems closely clad with unusually shaped leaves. Very pretty, but the flowers are tiny. 51♦

Centre left: Dolichothele (Mammillaria) longimamma
The extra-long tubercles make this cactus rather different from most mammillarias. Detached tubercles can be used for propagation. 52♦

Below left: Crassula arborescens
This can make a large shrub but it is also a good houseplant. It is best to take cuttings and restart when it becomes too large. 50♦

Below: Delosperma pruinosum (D. echinatum)
The tiny bristles of this delightful little succulent glisten like glass in the sunlight. Good light will keep it compact. 52♦

Above: **Echeveria derenbergii**
Being one of the most beautiful of the echeverias and also one of the easiest to grow makes this perhaps the ideal succulent. The brightly coloured flowers are carried on quite short stems. 53♦

Above right: **Echeveria gibbiflora** var. **carunculata**
A curious rather than beautiful plant grown mainly for the strange warty growths that appear on older leaves. When stems become 'leggy' restart by beheading. 54♦

Far right: **Echeveria harmsii**
The large flowers are really the showpieces of this echeveria and they are freely produced. The plant itself is straggly and is best kept under control by taking cuttings annually and restarting. 54♦

Right: **Echeveria 'Doris Taylor'**
A cultivated hybrid echeveria with beautiful velvety leaves and multicoloured flowers. Offsets often have roots while still on the parent plant, which makes propagation very easy. 53♦

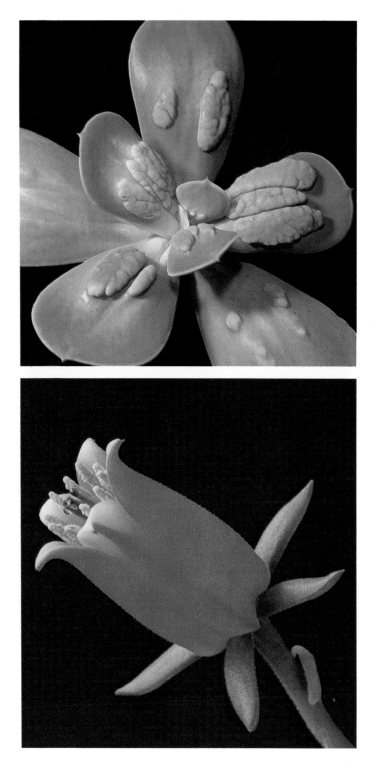

Top: **Echeveria setosa**
The compact hairy rosette of this succulent is attractive in itself apart from the magnificent array of flowers shown here. 55♦

Above: **Echinocactus grusonii**
Only really large specimens of this cactus will flower. Winter cold can cause brown markings, so best moved to a living-room. 56♦

Above:
Echinocereus pentalophus
*The sprawling stems of this cactus
are more than compensated for by
the large reddish-purple flowers
abundant even on small plants.* 57♦

Left:
Echinocereus horizonthalonius
*This cactus is a challenge to cultivate
but worth the effort.* 56♦

Below:
Echinocereus knippelianus
*A clump-forming cactus, easy to
grow and flower.* 57♦

Above: **Echinopsis multiplex**
The pink flowers of this easy cactus are unusual in that they are sweetly scented, but unfortunately they usually fade away after one or two days. The large flower and long tube are typical of echinopsis. 60♦

Above left:
Echinocereus perbellus
This small, globular cactus has a most distinctive spine formation and is worth growing for that alone. The large flowers are produced even on quite young plants. 58♦

Far left:
Echinocereus salm-dyckianus
One of the softer-stemmed echinocerei, this has more upright stems than most. Flowers well. 58♦

Centre left:
Epiphyllum 'Ackermannii'
Probably the most common and best epiphyllum hybrid in cultivation. 62♦

Left: **Epiphyllum 'Cooperi'**
Unusual among epiphyllum hybrids in producing flowers from the base. They are sweetly scented. 62♦

Above: **Echinopsis Paramount hybrid 'Peach Monarch'**
A vigorously growing echinopsis hybrid. The flowers have a beautiful satiny texture. 61♦

Left: **Echinopsis Paramount hybrid 'Orange Glory'**
This is probably the most strongly spined of the hybrid echinopsis. Radiant, large orange flowers. 61♦

Below:
Epiphyllum 'Deutsche Kaiserin'
A particularly floriferous hybrid with masses of pink blooms along the straplike stems. 63♦

Right: **Epiphyllum 'Gloria'**
*Epiphyllum hybrids are grown for
their flowers rather than for the
somewhat uninteresting stems. This
one produces truly immense blooms
in spring or summer, when it should
be shaded from full sunlight and
given an occasional feed.* 63♦

Below: **Euphorbia bupleurifolia**
*A particularly choice succulent
euphorbia. The flowers are small but
attractive, and the warty stems most
unusual. The male and female
flowers are on separate plants.
Never overwater this plant and make
sure drainage is good.* 64♦

Above right: **Euphorbia horrida**
*Euphorbia flowers are mostly small
and somewhat insignificant, but if
examined closely they are really
beautiful. Well worth using a
magnifier to study them.* 81♦

Right: **Euphorbia horrida**
*The resemblance to a cactus is only
superficial; this plant is a non-cactus
succulent. The sexes are on
separate plants, the presence of
pollen indicating a male.* 81♦

Far right: **Euphorbia mammillaris
var. variegata**
*The daintily variegated stems and
compact growth of this succulent
make it a most attractive plant,
though it has small flowers.* 81♦

Above: **Euphorbia milii**
Although not strictly a succulent, this euphorbia is certainly an 'honorary' one, as it is commonly included in collections and is a popular houseplant. In parts of the world where it can be grown outside all the year it makes a dense hedge; elsewhere it needs winter warmth. 82♦

Right: **Euphorbia resinifera**
One of the rather cactus-like succulents, which eventually forms quite a large clump. It is an easy plant to cultivate, provided it has a well-drained potting mixture and is kept dry in winter. Like all euphorbias, it has a milky sap that is extremely irritant. 83♦

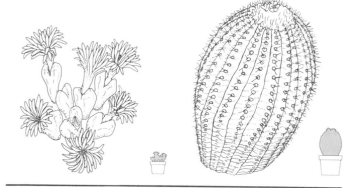

Conophytum frutescens

- Full sun
- Temp: 5-30°C (41-86°F)
- Give completely dry rest

Conophytum frutescens is sometimes listed under its old name of *C. salmonicolor*, which well describes the beautiful orange-pink flowers. The single pair of leaves is fused into a heart-shaped body about 3cm (1.2in) high. The leaves are green with light dots, and the flower emerges from the cleft in mid-summer. With age this plant develops stems, and ends up as a small shrub about 15cm (6in) high. If the plant seems to be deteriorating, remove the heads, leaving a short piece of stem attached to each head, and treat these as cuttings. Cuttings should be taken at the beginning of the growing period.

The soil should be very open: half loam-based mixture and half sharp sand or perlite. Repot every four or five years. During the resting period keep the plant completely dry; when the old plant body has completely shrivelled and the new heads have emerged (mid-summer), start watering, and continue until late autumn.

Take care
Keep the plant in full sun. 35♦

Copiapoa cinerea

- Full sun
- Temp: 5-30°C (41-86°F)
- Water cautiously

Copiapoa cinerea is one of the most beautiful cacti to come out of South America. It is grown for the beauty of its form; it rarely flowers in cultivation, probably because it is difficult to give it sufficient light to stimulate bud formation away from the burning sun of its native desert. Most plants seen in cultivation are the size of a grapefruit. It is chalky-white in colour, and the ribs carry glossy black spines that contrast beautifully with the white skin.

Copiapoas need very good drainage; use an open soil, of half loam-based mixture and half sharp sand or perlite. In the winter keep it dry, but during the summer water freely, allowing it to dry out between waterings. Keep this cactus in the sunniest part of the greenhouse; this will keep the plant brightly coloured.

With age, the plant will form offsets along the ribs. These may be used for propagation. *C. cinerea* looks more attractive when grown as a solitary plant.

Take care
Avoid damp winter conditions. 35♦

49

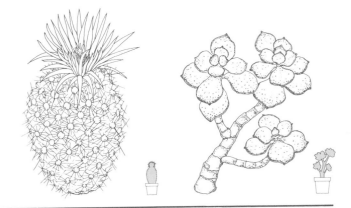

Coryphantha vivipara
- **Full sun**
- **Temp: 5-30°C (41-86°F)**
- **Water carefully**

Coryphanthas are small, globular cacti, very suitable for collectors with limited space. *C. vivipara* is a freely clustering plant; it is grey in colour and the stem is divided into tubercles. The tips of the tubercles carry white spines. The reddish flowers are borne on the top of the plant during the summer. The plant may be left as a cluster or some offsets used for propagation.

Any good potting mixture, either loam- or peat-based, may be used, with about one third of extra grit. During the late spring and summer, water freely, allowing the soil to dry out between waterings. Feed every two weeks with a high-potassium fertilizer when the buds form. Keep it dry in the winter. A sunny position is needed, because strong light stimulates bud formation and keeps the spines a good colour.

Mealy bug and root mealy bug are the pests most likely to be found; if so, water with a proprietary insecticide. If root mealy bugs are discovered, wash all the old soil off the roots and scrub the pot.

Take care
Do not let the soil get soggy. 36♦

Crassula arborescens
- **Full sun**
- **Temp: 5-30°C (41-86°F)**
- **Keep moist all the year**

Crassula arborescens is one of the largest of the crassulas, forming a shrub over 2m (6.5ft) high. It is an impressive background plant for a large greenhouse or may be used to decorate a paved area of the garden during the summer months. It has stout, woody stems, and the broad leaves are grey-green. The flowers are pink, but it is not an easy plant to flower; it is best regarded as a foliage plant.

A porous soil, consisting of two parts loam- or peat-based mixture and one part sharp sand or perlite, will ensure that the roots do not become waterlogged. This plant does not have a definite resting period and should be kept moist all the year. Crassulas require good light, but if the leaves start to look a little shrivelled, move the plant to a slightly shadier spot.

This plant is not greatly bothered by pests but scale insects can be a nuisance. They should be picked off by hand. If possible, avoid spraying, as this may mark the leaves.

Take care
Do not allow to dry out. 36♦

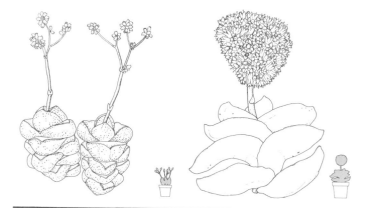

Crassula deceptrix
- **Full sun**
- **Temp: 7-30°C (45-86°F)**
- **Keep slightly moist all year**

This is a beautiful miniature plant, ideal for a small greenhouse or a sunny windowsill. The stems are 5cm (2in) high and are completely hidden by the closely packed leaves. The succulent leaves are covered with a white coating and the plant looks as if it were carved from white stone. The stems branch from the base. This is a slow-growing plant and may be kept in a 7.5cm (3in) pot for a number of years. The white bell-shaped flowers are carried on slender stems. It flowers freely in cultivation.

  C. deceptrix is easily propagated. Cut one of the stems, dry it for two days, and pot up. Although this species does not have a dry resting period, it should never be overwatered. A very porous mixture – one part loam-based potting medium and one part grit – is suitable; always allow it to dry out before watering again.

  White mealy bugs on a white plant can often remain unnoticed. Inspect regularly, and pick off any mealy bugs with forceps.

Take care
Water will mark the leaves. 37♦

Crassula falcata
- **Full sun**
- **Temp: 7-30°C (45-86°F)**
- **Keep moist all year**

Crassula falcata has such colourful flowers that it is a popular 'florist's plant' and is the parent of many beautiful hybrids. It is a small shrub, 30cm (12in) high. The large bluish-grey leaves are sickle-shaped. The stout flower stem carries a mass of tiny scarlet flowers; each individual flower is bell-shaped and they are arranged in a large, flat inflorescence. If the plant is grown in a greenhouse border, it will branch.

  The crassulas may be propagated from leaf or stem cuttings. Shrubby crassulas tend to become untidy with age and should be restarted in the early summer. Grow in a well-drained soil, two parts loam-based mixture to one part sharp sand or perlite. Keep moist all the year but allow to dry out between waterings and keep a little drier immediately after flowering. When the buds begin to form, feed with a liquid tomato fertilizer once every two weeks.

  This succulent makes quite a satisfactory houseplant if it can be given a window in full sun.

Take care
Restart leggy plants.

Delosperma pruinosum (D. echinatum)

- **Full sun**
- **Temp: 5-30°C (41-86°F)**
- **Keep moist all year**

Delosperma pruinosum is a small much-branched bush with plump, succulent leaves. These are covered with papillae, which have tiny bristles that give the leaves a glistening effect in the sun. The plant flowers continuously through the summer; the flowers, 1.5cm (0.6in) across, are whitish or yellow. The flowers open in the sunshine and close at night; they do not open on cloudy days or if the plant is in continuous shade.

D. pruinosum is most successfully grown in a sunny border where it can have a free root run. In climates where there is no danger of frost, it can be left outdoors permanently. Otherwise, take small cuttings during the summer, which can be wintered in a light position indoors. When it is grown outdoors the usual garden pests will be attracted and *D. pruinosum* can receive the same garden insecticides.

Take care
If grown as a pot plant, do not allow it to dry out. 37♦

Dolichothele (Mammillaria) longimamma

- **Full sun**
- **Temp: 5-30°C (41-86°F)**
- **Keep dry in winter**

Dolichothele longimamma is a free-flowering small plant, ideal where space is limited. The bright, glossy yellow flowers are 6cm (2.4in) across and are produced on and off all summer. The cactus itself is bright green with very pronounced tubercles, which have weak spines on their tips. The plant grows from a pronounced thickened tap root. With age, a few offsets are formed: these may be removed and used for propagation. *D. longimamma* can also be propagated from tubercles: remove a tubercle, dry it for two days, and pot up separately.

A good open mixture for this plant consists of two parts loam-based potting medium and one part sharp sand or perlite. During the spring and summer growing period water freely, but keep it dry during the winter. Sunlight is necessary to stimulate flower bud formation. Once the buds appear, water every two weeks with a high-potassium fertilizer.

Take care
Avoid cold, damp conditions. 37♦

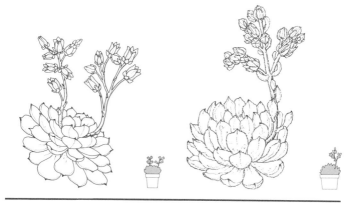

Echeveria derenbergii

(Painted lady)
- **Full sun**
- **Temp: 5-30°C (41-86°F)**
- **Keep moist all year**

Echeveria derenbergii is a charming small plant that does equally well in the greenhouse or on a sunny windowsill. It is a small, tightly leaved rosette, which forms offsets to make a small cushion. The bluish-grey leaves end in a red tip. The plant flowers freely during summer; the petals of the small bell-shaped flowers are yellow inside and orange outside.

 Echeverias are easy to cultivate, in a loam- or peat-based medium, with moderate watering in summer, plus a dose of high-potassium fertilizer every two weeks. In winter, keep slightly moist. In the wild, echeverias shed their lower leaves during the winter dry period, as a way of conserving moisture. In cultivation, even though the plant is not short of water, the lower leaves still shrivel, leaving a rather untidy plant in the spring. Remove the offsets and re-start the plants in early spring.

Take care
Do not let water collect in the centre of the rosette. 38♦

Echeveria 'Doris Taylor'

- **Full sun**
- **Temp: 5-30°C (41-86°F)**
- **Never allow to dry out**

Echeverias are such charming small pot plants that a number of hybrids have been developed. 'Doris Taylor' is a cross between *E. setosa* and *E. pulvinata.* It is a freely branching plant that looks its best in a half-pot. The pale green leaves are densely covered with white hairs and are carried on reddish-brown stems to form neat rosettes. The reddish-orange flowers are bell-shaped, and open in the spring.

 'Doris Taylor' should be grown in loam-based potting mixture in a light position – either in a greenhouse or on a windowsill. Water generously during spring and summer, and feed every two weeks with a high-potassium fertilizer. Keep slightly moist in winter. During the winter, the lower leaves shrivel: they should be removed or fungus will grow on them, which can cause the death of the plant. In spring, the plant will be leggy. Behead the main rosette and remove the smaller ones for potting.

Take care
Avoid cold, wet winter conditions. 38♦

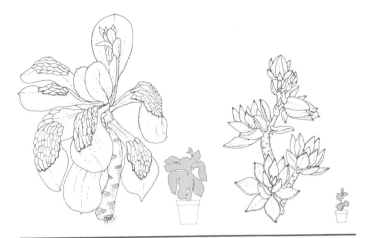

Echeveria gibbiflora
var. **carunculata**
- **Full sun**
- **Temp: 5-30°C (41-86°F)**
- **Keep slightly moist in winter**

Echeveria gibbiflora is one of the tall echeverias and seldom branches. The large leaves, 25cm (10in) long, are a lovely lavender-pink, and covered with large protuberances that are bluish to green. The protuberances are formed in autumn, so young plants may have completely plain leaves, but they will get their markings when autumn comes. The light red flowers open during the winter.

This plant tends to become leggy, and in the spring it should be beheaded. The base should be kept and with luck one or two offsets will form at the old leaf scars. These can be removed when about 2.5cm (1in) across and potted up. The top of the plant is, or course, also potted up. This is the only way to propagate this plant. Any good loam-based potting mixture may be used. Water generously during spring and summer. Keep just moist during the winter.

Take care
Do not splash the leaves with water, as it will mark the waxy coating. 39♦

Echeveria harmsii
- **Full sun**
- **Temp: 5-30°C (41-86°F)**
- **Keep moist all year**

Echeveria harmsii is the one echeveria that is grown for the beauty of its flowers rather than for its highly coloured leaves. The plant forms a small branching shrub with rosettes at the ends of the stems. These are made up of long, soft leaves covered in downy hair. The flowers are bell-shaped, 2.5cm (1in) long, and scarlet with a yellow tip.

Grow this plant in a loam- or peat-based potting mixture and keep it on a sunny windowsill. During summer, feed every two weeks with a high-potassium fertilizer and water generously, but give less water in the winter. If the plant looks untidy in spring, cut the rosettes off and treat as cuttings.

Echeverias are prone to harbour mealy bug. Pick the insects off, and if badly infested water the soil with a systemic insecticide. Since the plant is re-rooted every year, root mealy bug should not occur, provided the cuttings are planted in clean pots.

Take care
Do not let water collect in the centre of the rosettes. 39♦

Echeveria hoveyii
- Full sun
- Temp: 5-30°C (41-86°F)
- Water with caution

Echeveria setosa
- Full sun
- Temp: 5-30°C (41-86°F)
- Water with caution

Echeveria hoveyii is a pretty plant for a sunny windowsill or greenhouse. It consists of a cluster of loose rosettes on short stems. The long, narrow leaves are greyish-green with cream and pink stripes. The colour is at its brightest in spring. For really intense colour, keep in full sun and do not overwater. Occasionally the plant may grow a rosette without any markings; these should be removed.

Like many clustering plants, *E. hoveyii* looks its best when grown in a pan or bowl. Make sure there is a drainage hole. A loam- or peat-based growing medium with about one third extra grit is suitable for this plant. Allow to dry out between waterings.

During winter go over the plant weekly and remove any shrivelled leaves; if left on the plant, these can rot and become infected with fungus. In spring, the plant may well be untidy. Cut off the rosettes and re-root them. If any mealy bugs are seen, pick them off.

Take care
Remove any plain rosettes.

Echeveria setosa is a flat, almost stemless rosette about 15cm (6in) across. The soft, dark green leaves are covered with dense white hairs, which gives the plant an attractive furry appearance. This plant needs a sunny position. In the spring, mature specimens flower; the blooms are red and yellow.

The leaves of this echeveria are pressed very closely to the ground. Even in summer, the plant should be carefully inspected, and any shrivelled or rotting lower leaves removed. If left on, a grey mould will attack the decaying leaves.

A loam-based potting mixture will suit this plant, which should be grown in a half-pot. Water all the year round but allow it to dry out between waterings. When the flower buds start to form, feed every two weeks with a high-potassium (tomato) fertilizer. Mature specimens produce an occasional offset, which may be removed for propagation.

Take care
Do not allow water to collect in the centre of the rosette. 40♦

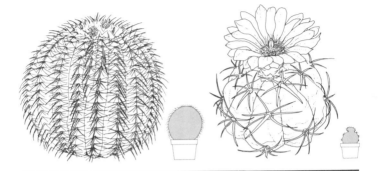

Echinocactus grusonii
(The golden barrel)
- Full sun
- Temp: 7-30°C (45-86°F)
- Keep dry in winter

Young specimens of *E. grusonii* have very pronounced tubercles and look like golden mammillaria. After a few years, the tubercles re-arrange themselves into ribs, usually about 28 per plant. *E. grusonii* is very long-lived and eventually reaches a diameter of 1m (39in). But in cultivation a plant of 15cm (6in) is a good-sized specimen and will be about 10 years old. The awl-shaped spines are pale golden-yellow and there is golden wool at the top of the plant. The small yellow flowers are produced on very large plants but only if exposed to very strong sunlight. In cooler climates, this plant is grown purely for the beauty of its colouring.

It needs an open soil, a loam- or peat-based mixture plus one third sharp sand or perlite. Water generously during summer, but allow it to dry out between waterings. Keep dry in winter. The chief pests are mealy bug and root mealy bug.

Take care
Avoid a cold, damp atmosphere. 40♦

Echinocactus horizonthalonius
- Full sun
- Temp: 7-30°C (45-86°F)
- Water with care

Echinocactus horizonthalonius is the baby of the genus, the only species that can be flowered in a pot. The flowers are pink and form a ring around the top of the plant. This cactus is a flattened plant, bluish-green in colour, with thick greyish spines. A flowering sized plant is 30cm (12in) across.

Although a very choice plant, *E. horizonthalonius* is not the easiest plant to cultivate. It is an extreme desert plant, and in its native state it bakes in the sun and has perfect drainage. The best treatment is to place the plant in the sunniest part of your greenhouse and grow it in a very open potting mixture. A loam-based mixture plus an equal quantity of sharp sand or perlite is suitable. Water on sunny days during spring and summer, but always allow the plant to dry out between waterings. Keep it dry during the winter.

Take care
Never allow to stand in water. 41♦

Echinocereus knippelianus
- Full sun
- Temp: 5-30°C (41-86°F)
- Keep dry in winter

Although this cactus may consist of a single oval or globular stem, about 5cm (2in) thick, for a few years, it will eventually form branches from the base, resulting in a compact clump. The stems have five ribs with a few short, bristly spines along them. Not being fiercely spined, it is quite an easy plant to handle. The deep pink flowers, 4cm (1.6in) or so across, appear from around the sides of the stems in spring and summer, and contrast delightfully with the dark green of the stems. Propagate this cactus by carefully cutting away a branch of at least 2.5cm (1in) across in spring or summer, letting it dry for a few days, and pushing it gently into fresh potting mixture.

Good drainage is essential, so grow this cactus in a mixture of two parts good standard potting material (peat- or loam-based) and one part sharp sand or perlite. When buds form, feed every two weeks with a high-potassium fertilizer.

Take care
Cut out any rotted branch. 41♦

Echinocereus pentalophus
- Full sun
- Temp: 5-30°C (41-86°F)
- Keep dry in winter

The small upright stem of this cactus soon branches and the ultimate result is a mass of sprawling shoots up to about 12cm (4.7in) long and 2cm (0.8in) thick. The spines are quite short and soft. On the whole perhaps it is not a particularly striking plant, but the magnificent blooms more than compensate for any lack of beauty in the cactus itself. Quite small specimens (one stem) will produce reddish-purple flowers up to 8cm (3.2in) across.

The stems, being rather soft and fleshy, are prone to rot with any excess water, so it is particularly important to use a well-drained potting mixture with no risk of waterlogging. Make this by adding one part of sharp sand or perlite to two parts of a standard potting mixture, which can be either peat- or loam-based. Propagate it by removing a suitable branch in summer, letting it dry for a few days, and potting up.

Take care
Water freely in summer. 41♦

Echinocereus perbellus

- **Full sun**
- **Temp: 5-30°C (41-86°F)**
- **Keep dry in winter**

One of the so-called 'pectinate' echinocerei, this shows a completely different type of stem from the more prostrate species. Here we have a predominantly solitary cactus, which may nevertheless form a low cluster with age. The stem is at first almost spherical and about 5cm (2in) across, but may eventually become more elongated. This stem is beautiful in itself; its many small ribs, closely decorated with short white spreading spines ('pectinate', or 'comb-like'), give a delightful, clean, neat appearance. The deep pink to purple flowers add to the attraction: about 5cm (2in) across, they open from hairy buds.

This cactus is almost completely hardy and can withstand dry freezing conditions in winter; but, to be on the safe side, keep to the recommended temperature, if possible. Grow it in a standard potting mixture to which has been added about one third of sharp sand or perlite.

Take care
Mealy bugs may hide among the spreading spines. 42♦

Echinocereus salm-dyckianus

- **Full sun**
- **Temp: 5-30°C (41-86°F)**
- **Keep dry in winter**

There are two types of echinocereus: those with fairly soft, mostly sprawling stems; and the pectinate (or comb-like) ones, with stiffer, elegantly spined, upright stems. This cactus belongs to the former group. Although small specimens consist of a single, upright stem, this soon branches at the base, eventually forming a clump of ribbed stems about 20cm (8in) long and 5cm (2in) thick, with short yellowish spines. It is probably the most attractive among the echinocerei, an attractiveness emphasized by the appearance of the funnel-shaped, pinkish flowers. These are about 7cm (2.8in) wide and can be up to 10cm (4in) long.

Grow in a mixture of one part sharp sand or perlite to two parts of any good standard material, to give the good drainage essential to this cactus. A gravel top dressing will protect the base. Feed every two weeks during the flowering season, to keep the flowers going.

Take care
Ensure a cold winter rest. 42♦

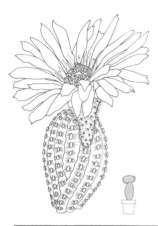

Echinocereus websterianus
- **Full sun**
- **Temp: 5-30°C (41-86°F)**
- **Keep dry in winter**

Another delightful echinocereus from the pectinate (comb-like) group. This cactus has a bright green stem divided into about 20 narrow ribs; along the length of each are groups of short, stiff, spreading white spines. In its native southern USA it can become quite large, but a good pot specimen would be about 15cm (6in) high and 5cm (2in) thick; branches are not usually formed. Blooms can be as wide as the plant itself, but usually on smaller specimens only one appears at a time, opening from a large bristly bud. The green and yellow centre of the flower contrasts splendidly with the lavender-pink petals.

Make up a well-drained potting mixture by adding one third of extra sharp sand or perlite to any good standard mix. With this you can water freely in spring and summer. Give this echinocereus a cold winter rest to ensure next year's flowers. If it is part of a living room collection, try to overwinter it in an unheated room.

Take care
Check for root loss in winter.

Echinofossulocactus lamellosus
- **Full sun**
- **Temp: 5-30°C (41-86°F)**
- **Keep dry in winter**

This group of cacti was formerly called *Stenocactus* and it is rather unfortunate that specialists have substituted the much longer name, if only because of the difficulty of writing it on a label! This is one of the prettiest, with a blue-green globular stem becoming rather cylindrical with age, and a diameter of up to 10cm (4in). The many thin ribs are wavy, which is characteristic of echinofossulocacti. White flattened spines are 1-3cm (0.4-1.2in) long, some curved upwards. This very attractive cactus will often produce its flowers when quite small; they are pink in colour, red inside, and tubular in shape, about 4cm (1.6in) long.

Coming as it does from sun-baked mountain regions, this plant can take all the sun you can give it in order to produce good spines and flowers. For this reason it is not so good as a houseplant. Water it freely in spring and summer, provided you grow it in a porous potting mixture of one part sharp sand or perlite to two parts soil.

Take care
Give this species a cold winter rest.

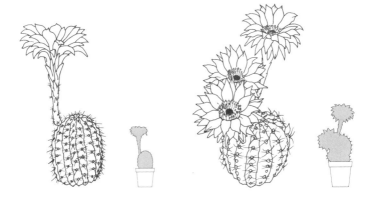

Echinopsis aurea
- Full sun
- Temp: 5-30°C (41-86°F)
- Keep cool and dry in winter

Echinopsis multiplex
- Full sun
- Temp: 5-30°C (41-86°F)
- Keep cool and dry in winter

Echinopsis aurea is still sometimes listed in catalogues under its old name of *Lobivia aurea*, which can be confusing. The plant has a cylindrical stem about 10cm (4in) high, which is ribbed, the ribs carrying short spines. A few offsets are formed on the main stem, and these may be removed and potted up.

The flowers are a beautiful lemon-yellow, which is an uncommon colour for an echinopsis. The main flush of flowers is in late spring, but odd flowers appear in summer.

Echinopsis plants need to be treated generously. Grow in loam-based mixture, which should be renewed annually. When buds appear, water once every two weeks with a liquid feed, the high-potassium type used for tomatoes. Like most desert cacti, *E. aurea* needs full sunlight to stimulate bud formation. Strong light also produces stout, well-coloured spines.

Take care
Feed generously when in bud, and during flowering.

The delicate pink flowers of this cactus open during the night and remain open during the following day. The flowers have a long tube about 20cm (8in) long and a sweet lily-like scent.

The genuine *E. multiplex* has long thick spines, but many pink-flowered echinopsis plants sold under this name are very short-spined hybrids, probably with *E. eyriesii*.

E. multiplex produces a profusion of offsets. To enable the main plant to reach flowering size quickly and to keep the plant within bounds, most of the offsets should be removed.

Large numbers of flowers are produced in early summer, and the plant should be fed during the flowering period with a tomato fertilizer. Any good potting mixture, either loam- or peat-based, is suitable for this species. Repot annually. Water freely during spring and summer, allowing the compost to dry out between waterings.

Take care
Watch for mealy bug. 43♦

Echinopsis Paramount hybrid 'Orange Glory'

- Full sun
- Temp: 5-30°C (41-86°F)
- Keep cool and dry in winter

'Orange Glory' is one of the beautiful *Echinopsis x Lobivia* hybrids that have been produced in the USA. The flowers are a deep glowing orange, a colour not found in pure echinopsis species. The cactus itself is cylindrical, with many ribs; the ribs carry short spines. A few offsets are produced on young plants; these may be left on the plant if a large specimen is desired, or removed for propagation.

This cactus may be grown in any loam- or peat-based mixture. Repot annually. Water freely during the spring and summer months, when the plant is in vigorous growth, but allow to dry out between waterings. When flower buds form feed every two weeks with a tomato fertilizer.

This is a desert plant and needs to be grown in full sunlight to stimulate bud formation and to encourage the growth of strong, well-coloured spines. This plant is tough and resistant to most pests.

Take care
Give plenty of sunshine. 44◗

Echinopsis Paramount hybrid 'Peach Monarch'

- Full sun
- Temp: 5-30°C (41-86°F)
- Feed while flowering

Echinopsis species have possibly the most beautiful flowers of any desert cacti, and among the most colourful are the hybrids developed in Paramount, California.

The peach-pink flowers of 'Peach Monarch' open during early summer, and there may be a dozen long-tubed flowers open at one time. Once the buds begin to form, the cactus should be kept moist and fed every two weeks. The best liquid feeds are those with a high potassium content.

'Peach Monarch' is 15cm (6in) high and 10cm (4in) across; short spines are carried on the numerous ribs. A few offsets are formed on young plants; use for propagation.

Echinopsis plants are easy to grow, in either a loam-based or a soilless compost. They are greedy plants, so repot annually. Give the plant a position where it will get maximum sunlight: strong light is necessary for bud formation.

Take care
Repot each year. 45◗

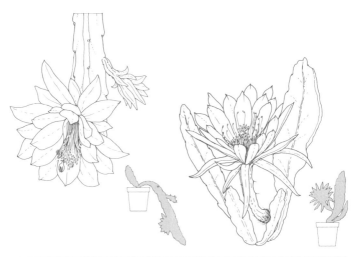

Epiphyllum 'Ackermannii'

(Orchid cactus)
- **Partial shade**
- **Temp: 5-27°C (41-81°F)**
- **Keep almost dry in winter**

Epiphyllums (also known as Epicacti) are among the most un-cactus-like cacti and are often grown by plant lovers who profess no interest in conventional cacti. Nevertheless, they are true cacti, but living naturally in tropical rain-forests rather than in the desert. Plants normally cultivated are hybrids between the various wild species and other cacti; such plants are hardier and have more colourful flowers. 'Ackermannii' is a typical example and is one of the oldest in cultivation, but its flowers have not been surpassed in beauty of colour. They are about 8cm (3.2in) across and brilliant red, but not perfumed. The blooms appear along the notched edges of the stems and may last for several days.

You can grow epiphyllums in a standard houseplant mixture, but if you add extra peat or leafmould to it, this is beneficial. Also, good drainage is important.

Take care
Feed with high-potassium fertilizer when in bud and flower. 43♦

Epiphyllum 'Cooperi'

(Orchid cactus)
- **Partial shade**
- **Temp: 5-27°C (41-81°F)**
- **Keep almost dry in winter**

The white flowers of this hybrid epiphyllum are perfumed; quite unusual for a cactus! Unlike those of other similar cacti, the flowers come from the base of the plant, not along the side of the stem. When the large buds are fully formed in spring or summer, they will open in the evening, and if they are in the living-room, a strong lily-like perfume will pervade the whole room at about 10pm. One can almost watch the buds unfold, to give brilliant white blooms maybe 10cm (4in) across.

This cactus will survive at the lower temperature in winter, but will do better if rather warmer. This is easy indoors, in a shady window. Water freely in spring and summer, and keep moister indoors in winter than in a greenhouse. But it appreciates a moist atmosphere; an occasional spray with water will help. Use a good standard potting mixture and feed occasionally.

Take care
Too much nitrogen in feed can cause brown spots. 43♦

Epiphyllum 'Deutsche Kaiserin'
(Orchid cactus)
- **Partial shade**
- **Temp: 5-27°C (41-81°F)**
- **Keep slightly moist in winter**

The parentage of many of the epiphyllum hybrids is somewhat obscure, and this one probably has no true epiphyllum ancestry at all, being a hybrid between two jungle cacti. But it is so like an epiphyllum in appearance and cultivation requirements that it is normally included with these plants. Most epiphyllums need staking when the stems reach a length of about 30cm (12in), but this one is really pendent, making it ideal for a hanging basket. In spring and summer the trailing stems, which may be up to 60cm (24in) long, are covered with masses of deep pink flowers, about 5cm (2in) across – a truly magnificent sight.

Grow this beautiful jungle cactus in a good standard potting mixture; if you add extra leafmould or peat it will be appreciated, as well as a feed every two weeks in spring and summer with a high-potassium fertilizer. Spray it occasionally and avoid full sunshine.

Take care
Never let this cactus dry out. 45♦

Epiphyllum 'Gloria'
(Orchid cactus)
- **Partial shade**
- **Temp: 5-27°C (41-81°F)**
- **Keep almost dry in winter**

There are literally dozens (if not hundreds) of epiphyllum hybrids available, and space prevents the mention of more than a few. But they all require much the same treatment. A good, nourishing potting mixture is important; add extra sharp sand or perlite if it looks at all compacted. Leafmould is not too readily available, but if you have any mix some with the potting mixture. Never add limestone or chalk. Never let the plant dry out completely, and water it freely in spring and summer, feeding every two weeks or so.

'Gloria' is a particularly attractive hybrid with immense orange-pink flowers up to 20cm (8in) across. But like those of most of the day-flowering types, these blooms are without scent. This hybrid is reasonably hardy, and a cool greenhouse is perfectly adequate. In the drier conditions of a living-room, an occasional spray with clean lime-free water is beneficial.

Take care
Keep out of full sunshine. 46♦

63

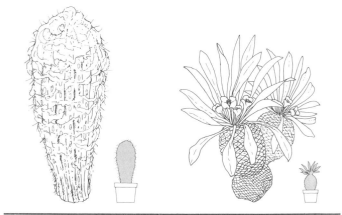

Espostoa lanata
- **Full sun**
- **Temp: 10-30°C (50-86°F)**
- **Keep dry in winter**

Although this cactus can reach tree-like proportions in its native state, 'seedling' plants are perfectly suitable for the collection, where they may reach a height of 30cm (12in) and a thickness of 5cm (2in) but will take many years to reach even this size. Specimens offered for sale are pretty little plants covered with a mass of white woolly hairs. It looks nice enough to stroke, but beware! Under the hair are needle-sharp spines; a trap for the unwary. As the cactus ages, these spines become larger and are visible outside the hair. Do not expect flowers; these are normally produced only on mature plants.

Grow in the usual well-drained potting mixture, made by adding about one third of sharp sand or perlite to a standard material. It is possible to overwinter this cactus in a cool greenhouse at a temperature of 5°C (41°F), but this is risky, and it is better to bring it indoors, unless it is already kept as a houseplant.

Take care
Plants in a window need to be turned.

Euphorbia bupleurifolia
- **Full sun**
- **Temp: 10-30°C (50-86°F)**
- **Keep dry in winter**

A choice, less common euphorbia, and although not one of the easiest to grow, it should not be too difficult for the careful collector. It is a small, spineless succulent, usually reaching a height of about 10cm (4in). The thick stem, which rarely branches, is covered with warty tubercles, and a tuft of leaves appears on the top during spring, and usually falls off at the approach of winter. The plant is grown more for its appearance than for the small flowers, which are produced in spring.

If greenhouse heating is kept low in winter, it is best to bring this plant indoors to an unheated room before any really cold weather, but put it in your lightest window.

Good drainage is essential for this plant, so add about one third of extra drainage material (sharp sand or perlite) to the potting mixture, which can be either loam- or peat-based. Water in spring and summer, but only when the soil is almost dry.

Take care
Avoid cold and wet conditions. 46▸

Top: **Euphorbia obesa**
An extreme succulent. This is a female plant with seed pods at the top of the single stem. 82♦

Above: **Faucaria tigrina**
An almost stemless succulent with pairs of leaves looking like tiny jaws. An easy plant to grow. 83♦

Top: **Ferocactus acanthodes**
*Normally only large specimens of
this cactus will flower, but the
colourful spines are beautiful.* 84♦

Above: **Ferocactus horridus**
*'Horridus' here means spiny, and
this cactus is very spiny indeed. Only
larger plants are likely to come into
flower. Never overwater.* 85♦

Above right: **Ferocactus latispinus**
*This ferocactus is quite likely to
flower, but usually only if the weather
is warm and sunny.* 85♦

Right: **Gasteria maculata**
*An ideal plant for the house or office
if given reasonable light, without full
sun, and not allowed to become
desiccated.* 87♦

Above: **Gymnocalycium bruchii**
A small, compact cactus, soon forming a freely flowering clump. This plant is sometimes listed in catalogues as G. lafaldense. 90♦

Right: **Gymnocalycium andreae**
The bright yellow flowers make this an unusual gymnocalycium. Single heads soon form offsets resulting in a neat clump. 89♦

Far left: **Glottiphyllum linguiforme**
Too much water will cause these succulents to become bloated rather than to rot, but they need enough to prevent shrivelling. Strike the happy medium and they are quite attractive plants with pairs of very fleshy leaves and magnificent flowers. They need plenty of light. 88▸

Left: **Gymnocalycium denudatum**
Sometimes known as the 'Spider Cactus' because of the short spreading spines clustered over its surface. The magnificent flowers are produced freely during spring and summer; they usually last for several days, and may be followed by seed pods. The seeds can be sown. 90▸

Below:
Gymnocalycium horridispinum
The unusually coloured flowers of this cactus make it outstanding even in this group of beautiful plants. Like most free-flowering desert cacti, this gymnocalycium needs a cool, dry winter rest in order to perform well the next year. Water in summer. 91▸

Above: **Gymnocalycium mihanovichii 'Hibotan'**
A novelty cactus that must always be grown on a graft, as it contains no food-making chlorophyll. Never let it become too cold. 91♦

Above right: **Haworthia maughanii**
One of the more unusual haworthias; it has flattened leaf tips, with transparent 'windows' to allow light to reach the inner tissues. In nature only the tips are exposed. 94♦

Far right: **Huernia zebrina**
The flowers are the chief attraction of this little succulent. They are large for such a small plant and most strange in appearance, with a slight, unpleasant smell. 95♦

Right: **Haworthia attenuata**
Haworthias make good houseplants as they enjoy reasonably shady conditions. Best grown under the staging in a greenhouse. 93♦

Above:
Kalanchoe daigremontiana
Tiny plantlets are freely produced along the edges of the leaves. The large mature leaves make this an impressive plant, but it is best to discard it and restart when it becomes straggly. 96♦

Right: **Kalanchoe blossfeldiana**
This is well-known as a houseplant. Its thickened leaves show that it is definitely a succulent. It produces masses of brilliant flowers in winter and spring. Restart it from cuttings if it becomes straggly. 95♦

Below: **Kalanchoe pumila**
A very free-flowering little succulent with pearly-grey leaves; the shade is due to their mealy coating. The thin stems eventually cause the plant to sprawl somewhat, making it very suitable for a hanging basket. 96♦

Left: **Lithops aucampiae**
Lithops or 'living stones' are extremely succulent plants, each head consisting of a pair of leaves without a stem. This is one of the larger species, with considerable variation in the leaf colour and pattern. Yellow flowers appear from between the leaves in autumn. A good, porous potting mixture is necessary and care in watering. 113♦

Below left: **Lithops bella**
The flower can be seen emerging from between the leaves in this photograph. *Lithops* do not have the range of flower colour found in the somewhat similar conophytums; they are either yellow or white. This one is slightly scented. The transparent 'windows' on top of the flattened leaves serve to admit light to the interior of the plant. In the wild these tops are level with the soil. 114♦

Below: **Lithops marmorata**
Surrounded by a mass of stones, this lithops would be difficult to find when not in flower; hence the term 'living stones' or 'stone mimicry plants' applied to this group in general. *Lithops* are easy plants to cultivate. Towards late autumn withhold all water and restart only in the spring when the old leaves have completely shrivelled away. New ones develop from the old. 115♦

Above: **Lobivia famatimensis**
Though it starts as a single stem, this attractive small cactus soon produces offsets from around the base to form a clump. Flower colour may vary from yellow to red. 116♦

Above left: **Lobivia backebergii**
The large, brilliant flowers of this lobivia make it a showpiece in any collection. The almost globular stem is usually solitary but sometimes offsets are formed at the base. It is a very easy cactus to grow. 115♦

Left: **Mammillaria bocasana**
The rounded, silky heads of this cactus and its ease of cultivation make it a popular mammillaria. But, beware! The silk conceals hooked spines, ready to catch on clothing. Easily raised from seed. 117♦

Above: **Mammillaria bombycina**
*One of the attractions of
mammillarias is the great variation of
shape and spine formation, not to
mention the usually freely produced
flowers. This species is not one of
the best for flowering, at least not in
the case of young plants, but its
delightful appearance more than
compensates, and the flowers are
small but beautiful.* 117♦

Above right:
Mammillaria zeilmanniana
*This is one of the most free-flowering
of all mammillarias; a complete ring
of blooms can be produced.* 119♦

Right:
Mammillaria zeilmanniana alba
*A white-flowered variety of the
species above. A clump of rounded
heads is eventually produced.* 119♦

Above:
Neoporteria mammillarioides
Large flowers are freely produced at *the top of this beautifully spined* *cactus and they may last for a week.* *Needs a cold winter rest.* 121♦

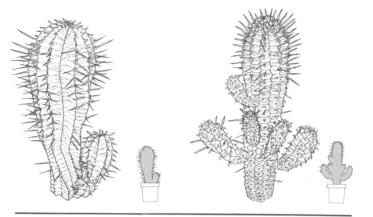

Euphorbia horrida
- Full sun
- Temp: 5-30°C (41-86°F)
- Keep dry in winter

Although a very cactus-like plant, this is one of the 'other succulents'. The very small flowers and stout spines (not needle-like) give it away. It is not a 'horrid' plant; the name *horrida* means 'spiny'. In its native South Africa it can reach quite a large size, but a good cultivated specimen is not likely to be more than about 20cm (8in) high and 5cm (2in) thick. The attraction of this succulent is more in its shape than in its tiny flowers, although when clustered at the top these can be quite pretty. Plants are male or female.

E. horrida can be propagated from seed (but remember you need a pair) or from the branches that sometimes form at the base. If you remove the branches, wash off the oozing latex and let the cutting dry for a week before potting up. For this plant use a mixture of three parts standard soil and one part sharp sand or perlite.

Take care
Keep any white latex away from your eyes or mouth. 46-7♦

Euphorbia mammillaris var. **variegata**
(Corn cob)
- Full sun
- Temp: 5-30°C (41-86°F)
- Keep dry in winter

A beautifully variegated form of *E. mammillaris* (itself an attractive little succulent), this plant attains a height of around 20cm (8in) and a thickness of 5cm (2in). Grow it for its form and colour rather than its insignificant flowers. The freely produced branches soon give rise to a small bush of deeply ribbed stems, variegated with white, on which the blunt spines appear in bands.

If you want to propagate this euphorbia, remove a branch, wash off the sappy latex, and let it dry for a week before planting. A pity to spoil the look of the plant, but sometimes an ill-positioned branch can be found. To grow this euphorbia well, use any good standard potting mixture with about one third of sharp sand or perlite added. With the consequent good drainage, watering can be quite liberal during spring and summer.

Take care
Keep the latex away from your eyes or mouth. 47♦

Euphorbia milii var. splendens
(Crown of thorns)
- Full sun
- Temp: 10-30°C (50-86°F)
- Keep slightly moist in winter

This delightful little shrub, only slightly succulent, is very popular as a houseplant, and deservedly so, as it is more suited to a well-lit living-room window in winter than to the average colder greenhouse, where it will certainly lose its long leaves, and probably its life also!

The plant's great attraction is its brilliant scarlet flower-like bracts, about 1.5cm (0.6in) across, produced freely in spring and summer. There is also a yellow version.

If the stems become too long, encourage more bushy growth by cutting them down to size; this also provides ample cuttings for spare plants. Keep any sap away from your eyes or mouth. Let the pieces dry for a few days and pot up; they should root fairly easily in spring and summer. Grow this euphorbia in any good loam- or peat-based potting mixture, and water freely in spring and summer.

Take care
Avoid cold draughts in winter. 48♦

Euphorbia obesa
- Full sun
- Temp: 5-30°C (41-86°F)
- Keep dry in winter

A true succulent in every sense of the word; there could hardly be a greater difference between this euphorbia and the preceding one. It has a most distinctive spineless, leafless greyish-green stem with a pale purple pattern. At first almost spherical and up to about 7cm (2.8in) across, it usually becomes taller with age. Having neither offsets nor branches, propagation is only from seed, which requires both male and female plants, as the sexes are separate. Tiny flowers with a delightful, delicate perfume are formed at the top of the plant, and followed by seed pods in the case of a female plant that has been pollinated.

Grow this attractive novelty in a well-drained medium consisting of two thirds of a standard potting mixture and one third sharp sand or perlite. This euphorbia tends to have a long tap root, so use a fairly deep pot for it.

Take care
Water in spring/summer only. 65♦

Euphorbia resinifera
- Full sun
- Temp: 5-30°C (41-86°F)
- Keep dry in winter

This is probably the oldest known succulent plant of all, having been discovered by an eastern king about 25BC! In cultivation it is a low, much-branched shrub, with four-angled bright green stems up to 30cm (12in) high. There are short spines in pairs along the edges of the branches. Flowers are seldom or never produced on cultivated plants, but if they were, they would be tiny and rather insignificant. Branches can be cut away and used for propagation, but the cut ends 'bleed' profusely with a white milky sap; this should be washed off with water and the branch allowed to dry for a week. Do this only during spring and summer.

Grow this euphorbia in a good, well-drained potting mixture of three parts standard peat- or loam-based material with one part of sharp sand or perlite. Water it quite freely in spring and summer but then gradually reduce for its winter rest.

Take care
Keep any trace of the white sap away from eyes or mouth. 48♦

Faucaria tigrina
(Tiger's jaws)
- Full sun
- Temp: 5-30°C (41-86°F)
- Keep almost dry in winter

Faucarias are not only pretty, but also easy to grow. These small succulents will grow on a sunny windowsill or in a sunny greenhouse. *F. tigrina* is a low-growing plant consisting of rather crowded succulent leaves, each of which has an edging of 'teeth'. The leaves are grey-green in colour, and covered with tiny white dots. The large golden-yellow flowers appear in autumn; they open in the afternoon if it is sunny, and close at night.

If overwatered, faucarias tend to become too large. Grow them in a soil consisting of half loam-based material and half sharp sand or perlite. Water freely in summer, but allow them to dry out in between. Give only an occasional watering in winter. With age, faucarias develop pronounced woody stems. In late spring, cut the heads off, with about 0.5cm (0.2in) of stem, and dry for a day before potting up.

Take care
It is not necessary to repot more than once every three years. 65♦

Fenestraria rhopalophylla
- ● Full sun
- ● Temp: 5-30°C (41-86°F)
- ● Completely dry in winter

Fenestraria rhopalophylla has grey-green cylindrical leaves that end in a transparent 'window'. In the desert regions of south-west Africa, the leaves are buried in the ground up to their tips and the light is filtered down to the chlorophyll through the 'window'. In cultivation the plant is grown completely above ground, partly because of the poorer light and also to prevent rotting.

The leaves, about 2.5cm (1in) long, grow in little clusters. The plant is vigorous and will soon fill a pan. The growing period starts early in spring and continues through the summer. White flowers appear in summer; they open in the sunshine and close again at night.

Grow in a sandy soil. It does not need repotting annually; when potting on, be careful not to disturb the roots. Water freely during spring and summer but keep completely dry during autumn and winter. Propagate by removing the heads during early summer.

Take care
Allow to dry out between waterings.

Ferocactus acanthodes
- ● Full sun
- ● Temp: 5-30°C (41-86°F)
- ● Keep dry in winter

'Ferocactus' means 'ferocious cactus' and this aptly describes these plants, with their array of sharp, tough spines. *F. acanthodes* is a particularly attractive member of the group. It is spherical, becoming more elongated with age, and the many ribs are furnished with reddish spines up to 4cm (1.6in) long, some of them curved. A giant cactus in nature, it is slow-growing and perfectly suitable as a pot specimen; in a pot it can attain a diameter of 15cm (6in) or more, but takes years to do so. However, small plants do not usually flower.

Ferocacti are particularly sensitive to insufficient light and overwatering, so give this one all the direct sunshine you can, and add extra drainage material to a standard peat- or loam-based potting mixture (one part to two parts mixture). It is best to water only when the mixture has almost dried out. A top dressing of grit or gravel will keep the base dry.

Take care
Watch for drips in the greenhouse; they could be fatal! 66♦

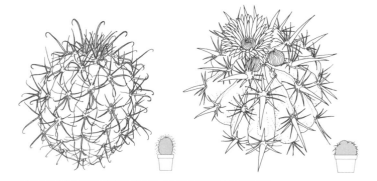

Ferocactus horridus
- **Full sun**
- **Temp: 5-30°C (41-86°F)**
- **Keep dry in winter**

A fiercely armed cactus with an almost globular stem – which in cultivation is unlikely to exceed a diameter of 10cm (4in) – divided into about 12 ribs. Very strong, reddish spines occur in groups along the ribs, up to 5cm (2in) long; the longest spine in each group is flattened and hooked at the tip. Ideally designed to catch in the clothing and pull the plant off the staging! Although yellow flowers can be produced, they are unlikely on smaller plants, so it is best not to hope for them, but to be content with the plant itself.

Grow this ferocactus in a porous potting mixture, which you can make up by adding one part of sharp sand or perlite to two parts of a standard material, and mixing it thoroughly. It is best to water only on sunny days in summer, to avoid any risk of the potting mixture becoming too wet. If the plant should lose its roots, cut it back to clean tissue and allow to dry out for a few days before replanting.

Take care
To handle, wrap it in a thick fold of newspaper! 66♦

Ferocactus latispinus
- **Full sun**
- **Temp: 5-30°C (41-86°F)**
- **Keep dry in winter**

Probably the best-known of the ferocacti, and if you want only one from this group, this is the one to choose. Unlike most of the others, which usually need to reach massive proportions before flowering, this is a species that should burst into bloom when it reaches a diameter of about 10cm (4in). The flowers, 4cm (1.6in) across, are a beautiful purple-red in colour, and open in succession from autumn until early winter. But here lies the snag: unless the autumn is warm and sunny, the buds will probably not open at all! The deeply indented ribs of the bright green stem bear rows of strong, deep yellow spines, some flattened and tipped with red; the whole plant when in flower is a magnificent sight.

As with other ferocacti, a well-drained potting mixture is essential; one part of sharp sand or perlite mixed into two parts of a standard material will prevent any risk of waterlogging, often fatal.

Take care
Keep in the sunniest place. 67♦

85

Frailea castanea
- **Full sun**
- **Temp: 5-30°C (41-86°F)**
- **Keep dry in winter**

This one is a real dwarf cactus, a good-sized specimen being only about 4cm (1.6in) across and almost spherical in shape. Formerly known as *F. asteroides*, it is rather like a miniature version of the cactus *Astrophytum asterias* in appearance, though not in size or in colouring, as it is a greyish bronze. The slightly flattened plant body has a number of blunt ribs; the tiny clumps of spines are more a decoration than a menace. This little cactus flowers quite readily in spring and summer but fraileas exhibit an unusual phenomenon in that the flowers are mostly self-pollinated without opening. Occasionally, however, on a really sunny day the flowers open normally; they are yellowish.

Grow *Frailea castanea* in a mixture of standard material and sharp sand or perlite in proportions of about three to one. With such a small plant, you are never likely to need a pot larger than 5cm (2in). A top dressing of grit will protect the plant base.

Take care
Very small pots dry out easily.

Frailea knippeliana
- **Full sun**
- **Temp: 5-30°C (41-86°F)**
- **Keep dry in winter**

There are two types of fraileas; those with globular stems and those with more elongated stems. This little cactus is one of the latter. It is a true miniature with a bright green stem only about 4cm (1.6in) high and 2.5cm (1in) thick and it does not normally produce offsets. The flowers are prettily marked in red and yellow but are only likely to open in full sun; the plant is quite capable of pollinating itself.

You may come across other fraileas; they are all minute plants, needing very much the same method of cultivation, which is quite easy, and their size makes them ideal for the smallest space on a windowsill or greenhouse staging. Either peat- or loam-based potting mixture is suitable, but it is well to increase the drainage by mixing in one third to one quarter of sharp sand or perlite. Water all fraileas quite freely in spring and summer, but reduce watering towards the autumn, ready for the winter rest.

Take care
Avoid damp, cold conditions.

Gasteria batesiana
- Partial shade
- Temp: 5-30°C (41-86°F)
- Keep slightly moist in winter

Among the most shade-loving of succulents, gasterias make ideal houseplants, or occupy that space under the greenhouse staging that is not always easy to make full use of. They are best kept out of full sun, or the usually cheerful green colouration may take on an unhealthy reddish tinge. *G. batesiana* has very thick, triangular-sectioned leaves arranged in a stout rosette. They are an olive-green colour spotted with raised white dots. Offsets are usually formed eventually, making propagation quite easy. Often these already have roots and it is merely necessary to pull one or more away and pot up straight away. Don't spoil a nice-looking clump, but you may have to remove some anyway to prevent the clump from becoming larger than you want. The pinkish-red tubular flowers are small and grouped along a stem.

Use a good, well-drained potting mixture, and water quite freely in spring and summer, reducing towards winter.

Take care
Mealy bugs hide between leaves.

Gasteria maculata
- Partial shade
- Temp: 5-30°C (41-86°F)
- Keep slightly moist in winter

Probably the most popular of the gasterias, this succulent is often to be seen in home and office windows, where its very existence is a tribute to its ability to survive adverse conditions! It is one of the easiest of succulents to grow, but so frequently ill-treated. Just water it freely in spring and summer and give it something nourishing to live in, and it will reward you with an appearance quite different from its ill-treated relatives. The flattened leaves are about 15cm (6in) long and 4cm (1.6in) wide, glossy green with white spots or bands. They form two rows, rather than a rosette, at least in younger plants. Offsets are freely produced, soon forming a clump, which will probably have to be split up eventually, unless it can be grown in a wide pan.

This gasteria will survive at 5°C (41°F) in winter if it is quite dry, but it is happier at a rather higher temperature and moister, in a living-room or kitchen. It may be outdoors in summer.

Take care
Avoid full sun and dark corners. 67♦

Glottiphyllum arrectum

- Full sun
- Temp: 5-30°C (41-86°F)
- Water with great caution

Glottiphyllums are pretty little South African plants that are easy to grow. But if overwatered, they lap the water up and turn into bloated monstrosities.

G. arrectum has two or three pairs of semi-cylindrical leaves, which are 5cm (2in) long and bright green. During summer, the leaves develop a pretty purplish colour. The shining golden-yellow flowers are about 7cm (2.8in) across and are formed in early winter; they open in the late afternoon and close at night, and they open for several days running, provided the sun shines. The side shoots may be used for propagation.

To prevent obesity, glottiphyllums should be grown in a mixture that is half grit; repot every three or four years. The growing period is from late summer to late autumn. During this period water the plant, allowing it to dry out between waterings. Otherwise, the plant should be kept dry. Keep it in a very light position.

Take care
Never overwater.

Glottiphyllum linguiforme

- Full sun
- Temp: 5-30°C (41-86°F)
- Water with great caution

Glottiphyllum linguiforme is an attractive plant, provided it is not overwatered. It will mop up any amount of water, becoming more and more distorted in the process. This glottiphyllum has two rows of thick tongue-like leaves, which are 5cm (2in) long, and bright shiny green in colour. The plant blooms on sunny days in late autumn or early winter. Like many South African succulents, its shining yellow flowers open on sunny days and close at night. The plant will form side shoots, which may be removed for propagation during the latter half of the summer.

A good potting mixture is half loam-based medium and half sharp sand or perlite. The plant should be repotted every third or fourth year. During late summer and autumn, water on sunny days, allowing it to dry out between waterings. Watch for mealy bugs, which are the main pest. Spraying with a proprietary insecticide will eliminate them.

Take care
Grow in a sunny position. 68♦

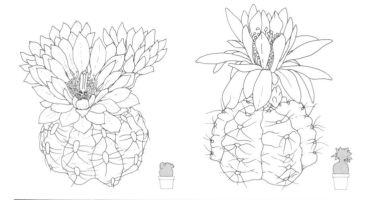

Gymnocalycium andreae

- Full sun
- Temp: 5-30°C (41-86°F)
- Keep dry in winter

Most gymnocalyciums are fairly small, compact cacti, very suitable for the average collection, but this one is particularly desirable as it only reaches a diameter of about 5cm (2in), although a small clump is eventually formed. The spines, some of which are curved, are quite short. This little plant is very free-flowering, producing its bright yellow blooms, about 3cm (1.2in) across, in spring and summer. The colour is unusual for a gymnocalycium, which mostly have white or greenish-white flowers. Offsets soon appear on the main plant; they can be removed for propagation, or left on to produce eventually a rounded mass of beautifully flowering heads.

Full sun is needed, and any good potting mixture may be used, either loam-based or loamless. But good drainage is essential and about one third of extra sharp sand or perlite should be added. During late spring and summer water freely but let the plant become almost dry first.

Take care
Watch out for the mealy bug pest. 68▸

Gymnocalycium baldianum

- Full sun
- Temp: 5-30°C (41-86°F)
- Keep dry in winter

Like *Gymnocalycium andreae* this cactus is different from the general run of gymnocalyciums in the colour of its flowers, in this case a brilliant red, although pink-flowered versions are to be found. It is sometimes met under its former name of *G. venturianum*, which may lead to some confusion when looking through nurserymen's lists. The stem is a bright green ball with a diameter of about 7cm (2.8in) and seldom produces offsets. The well-rounded ribs show the typical gymnocalycium notches or 'chins'. Well-treated plants produce beautiful flowers, about 4cm (1.6in) across, in spring and summer. Like most cacti, this one will give of its best in a greenhouse, but there is no reason why it should not be grown and flowered on a sunny windowsill.

Use a good, well-drained potting mixture, as for the preceding species, and feed every two weeks with a high-potassium fertilizer during spring and summer.

Take care
Avoid damp and cold conditions.

Gymnocalycium bruchii

- **Full sun**
- **Temp: 5-30°C (41-86°F)**
- **Keep dry in winter**

Another small-growing cactus, and if one had to choose a single beauty, easily obtainable, from among a lovely group, this could well be it. But it has a confusing alias; it is sometimes called *G. lafaldense*, so take care not to buy the same plant twice! A small compact clump of neatly spined, rounded heads is soon formed, which produces pinkish blooms very freely. Far better to leave this cactus as a clump, but often the heads become so crowded that a few can be removed to make room for the others. Carefully cut them away with a thin knife, allow them to dry off for a few days and just press them into fresh potting mix in late spring and summer.

Either loam- or peat-based potting mixture may be used, but increase the drainage by mixing in about one third of sharp sand or perlite. Watering can be quite free in spring and summer, and every two weeks or so give a dose of fertilizer.

Take care
Mealy bugs hide between heads. 68♦

Gymnocalycium denudatum

(Spider cactus)
- **Full sun**
- **Temp: 5-30°C (41-86°F)**
- **Keep dry in winter**

This is perhaps the best-known gymnocalycium and more or less typical of the whole group. It is an almost globular cactus reaching the size of about 15cm (6in) across and 10cm (4in) high. The deep green plant body or stem is furnished with broad ribs and the notches along them give the typical 'chin' effect, although this is less pronounced than in other similar plants. The popular name of 'Spider cactus' refers to the short spreading spines, somewhat resembling small spiders crawling over the plant. Beautiful greenish-white or pinkish flowers add to the attractiveness of this cactus during spring and summer. They are about 5cm (2in) across.

Grow this cactus in a potting mixture of about two thirds standard growing medium and one third sharp sand or perlite and feed occasionally with a high-potassium fertilizer during the bud and flower stage.

Take care
Make sure the winter dryness is not spoilt by greenhouse drips! 69♦

Gymnocalycium horridispinum

- **Full sun**
- **Temp: 5-30°C (41-86°F)**
- **Keep dry in winter**

One of the attractions of gymnocalyciums is their great variety of shape, spines and flowers, and this one is indeed a beauty among them. It is rather less typical of the group as a whole, being more elongated than globular; an average-sized plant is about 13cm (5in) tall and 8cm (3.2in) broad. Also it has delightful pink flowers up to 6cm (2.4in) across. In spite of their size, three or four flowers can be produced at a time, and they may last for up to a week. Unfortunately, they have no perfume! There are well-formed 'chins' along the ribs of the bright green stem and these bear stout, spreading spines, about 3cm (1.2in) long. Incidentally, its Latin name does not mean 'horrid', but 'prickly' or 'spiny'.

Grow this lovely plant in the usual well-drained standard potting mixture with extra sharp sand or perlite, and feed occasionally in spring and summer.

Take care
Avoid soggy potting mixture. 69♦

Gymnocalycium mihanovichii 'Hibotan'

- **Partial shade**
- **Temp: 10-30°C (50-86°F)**
- **Keep dryish in winter**

Looking something like a tomato on a stick, this cactus, sometimes also called 'Ruby Ball', is certainly unusual. It was first developed in Japan. Some cacti suppliers incorrectly call it the 'everlasting flower'. But the top is no flower, simply an abnormal version of *G. mihanovichii*, lacking chlorophyll. Consequently this novel cactus must always be grown grafted.

A tender jungle cactus, hylocereus, identified by its three-cornered stem, is most often used as a grafting stock; unless you can keep a winter temperature of at least 10°C (50°F), it is better to re-graft onto something tougher, such as a trichocereus. Otherwise treat 'Hibotan' as a houseplant, for which it is ideally suited. You may be rewarded with attractive white or pink flowers. Use a potting mixture of three parts of a standard material and one part of sharp sand or perlite, and be careful never to overwater.

Take care
Avoid full summer sun. 70♦

91

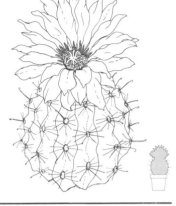

Gymnocalycium quehlianum
- Full sun
- Temp: 2-30°C (36-86°F)
- Keep dry in winter

Probably the most common gymnocalycium, and one of the hardiest. It is an ideal beginner's cactus. Large, lustrous flowers, up to 6cm (2.4in) across, white with pink centres, are abundantly produced, even on small plants. The plant is a flattened sphere, about 10cm (4in) across and 6cm (2.4in) high when fully grown, with deep rounded ribs and pronounced 'chins'. Offsets are rarely produced and the yellowish, curved spines are quite short. Although individual flowers last for only a day or two, a succession means that this fine cactus is in bloom for several weeks during spring and summer.

Water quite freely from spring until late summer, and use a high-potassium fertilizer about once every two weeks when the plant is in bud and flower. Add about one third of sharp sand or perlite to any good standard peat- or loam-based potting mixture.

Take care
Never let water collect in the depressed top of the plant.

Hamatocactus setispinus
- Full sun
- Temp: 5-30°C (41-86°F)
- Water freely during summer

This small cactus does particularly well in cultivation; plants only 2.5cm (1in) across will flower. The yellow blooms have a deep red throat and are borne on the top of the plant during summer. An adult plant is about 13cm (5in) across, with a dark green skin and white spines.

A suitable growing medium for this plant is two parts loam- or peat-based mixture to one part of sharp sand or perlite. Repot annually and inspect the roots for the grey ashy deposits that indicate the presence of root mealy bug. If found, wash the old soil off the roots and repot into a clean container. The plant should be watered freely during the summer months but allowed to dry out between waterings; keep it dry during the winter. Full sun is necessary to stimulate flowering and to encourage the growth of long stout spines. Feed every two weeks with a high-potassium fertilizer when flower buds start to appear.

Take care
Make sure drips in the greenhouse do not spoil winter dryness.

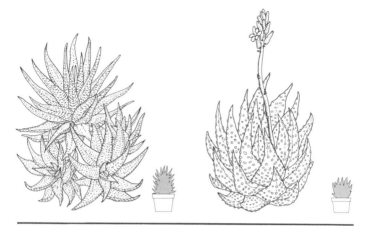

Haworthia attenuata
- **Partial shade**
- **Temp: 5-30°C (41-86°F)**
- **Keep slightly moist in winter**

In their native Africa, haworthias receive shade from the larger plants among which they are growing. If exposed to very strong light, the leaves become unattractively bronzed. In a greenhouse they thrive in shady corners or under the staging – places where most succulent plants become distorted because of the poor light. They also do very well as room plants; their tolerance of partial shade and their small size make them ideal.

Haworthia attenuata forms a stemless rosette of tough, dark green leaves. These have bands of white tubercles, which glisten attractively. Haworthias are all grown for the beauty of their form, not for their flowers; the tiny white bells are carried on the end of long straggly stems.

Grow this species in half-pots, in a loam-based potting mixture, and repot annually. With age *H. attenuata* will form offsets, which can be removed and used for propagation.

Take care
Avoid strong sunshine. 70♦

Haworthia margaritifera
- **Partial shade**
- **Temp: 5-30°C (41-86°F)**
- **Keep slightly moist in winter**

Haworthia margaritifera is a stemless rosette about 15cm (6in) in diameter, consisting of dark green curved leaves, frosted with prominent pearly tubercles. Some plants are more prettily marked than others; if possible, choose your plant personally. The flowers are small white bells, carried on the end of long wiry stems.

This plant grows best in partial shade. It does well as a houseplant, or it will fill in a shady corner of the greenhouse. If grown indoors, occasionally wash the leaves to remove any dust.

Use a loam-based potting mixture and grow in a half-pot. Haworthias have thick, shiny white roots. During the resting period these shrivel and the plant grows a new set of roots. If you repot in the early summer you may well find that the plant has little root, but this is quite natural. Haworthias tend to grow and flower well into the winter, and rest during the spring.

Take care
Do not let it dry out completely.

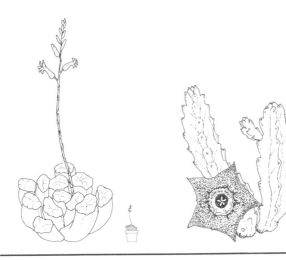

Haworthia maughanii
- **Diffuse sunlight**
- **Temp: 5-30°C (41-86°F)**
- **Water with caution**

This is one of the choicest haworthias. The semi-cylindrical leaves are arranged in rosettes. The leaves are about 2.5cm (1in) long, and look as if someone had sliced the tip of the leaf off. The leaves have 'windows' at the ends. In their native desert the leaves are buried with only the tips showing, and light is filtered into the plant through the exposed 'windows'. However, in cultivation the plant is grown completely above the soil, to prevent rotting. The leaves are dark green, and the plant flowers during early winter, producing small white bells.

A growing medium consisting of one half loam-based potting mixture and one half sharp sand or perlite will ensure that the plant does not become too wet. Always allow it to dry out between waterings. This is a very slow-growing plant and will live in a 7.5cm (3in) pot for many years. During the resting period, the thick contractile roots will shrivel and be replaced by new ones.

Take care
Never overwater. 71♦

Huernia aspera
- **Full sun**
- **Temp: 5-30°C (41-86°F)**
- **Keep almost dry in winter**

Huernia aspera is a neat little succulent plant, related to the much larger stapelias. The freely branching, bright green stems are only about 8cm (3.2in) long and 1.5cm (0.6in) in thickness. They are angled with soft teeth, but no leaves. The purple-red flowers are five pointed and very fleshy, 2cm (0.8in) across, with little or no odour.

All stapelia-type succulents tend to be rather touchy with regard to watering and temperature, but this is one of the easiest and most hardy, surviving quite happily in a cool greenhouse in winter, with only enough dampness in the potting mixture to prevent it from shrivelling unduly. It also makes a good little specimen for the living-room windowsill. But it cannot tolerate overwatering; ensure a well-drained potting mixture by adding one part of sharp sand or perlite to two parts of a standard material. To water, dip the pot, remove it, and allow it to drain.

Take care
Watch for black marks in winter – a sign of rot, or infection.

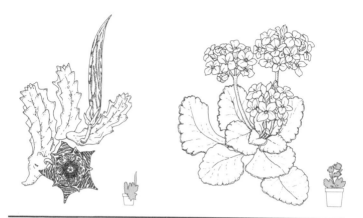

Huernia zebrina
- **Full sun**
- **Temp: 5-30°C (41-86°F)**
- **Keep almost dry in winter**

The name refers to the zebra-like
stripes on the flowers of this
miniature succulent — if a zebra
could have purple-brown stripes on
a yellow background! But, accurate
or not, this flower is delightfully
attractive and unusual. The five
striped lobes surround a thick purple
central ring, the whole flower being
about 4cm (1.6in) across. There is
almost no smell, but what little there
is is unpleasant, characteristic of
most of the stapelia-type succulents!
The plant itself consists of sharply
toothed, angled stems, bright green
in colour and around 8cm (3.2in)
long and 2cm (0.8in) thick.

Grow this huernia in a mixture of
two parts of a standard material and
one part of sharp sand or perlite.
Never allow the potting mixture to
become too wet, or rot or infection
can set in. This is indicated by black
marks, or black tips to the stems. In
winter, give only enough water to
prevent severe shrivelling, but in
spring and summer water freely.

Take care
Treat black marks with fungicide. 71♦

Kalanchoe blossfeldiana
- **Good light**
- **Temp: 10-27°C (50-81°F)**
- **Keep slightly moist in winter**

This succulent is undoubtedly a
houseplant, although it can certainly
be grown in a greenhouse. Many
horticultural hybrids are on the
market, as they are popular florists'
plants, usually being available in
autumn and winter in full bloom. A
typical specimen would be up to
30cm (12in) high with wide, thick
bright green leaves, but the plants
offered for sale are usually smaller.
This is predominantly a flowering
plant, producing masses of bright
red flowers from autumn until spring.
The flowers are individually small,
but they are clustered in tight heads,
giving a brilliant display of colour.
There is a yellow-flowered variety.

Never overwater this plant, as the
stems are prone to rot off, but never
let it dry out completely either.
However, in a good, well-drained
potting mixture it is easy to cultivate;
mix some extra sharp sand or perlite
with a standard material to improve
the drainage. Take stem cuttings in
spring; pot them straight away.

Take care
Full summer sun can scorch. 73♦

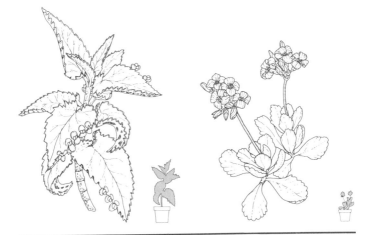

Kalanchoe daigremontiana
- **Full sun**
- **Temp: 10-27°C (50-81°F)**
- **Keep slightly moist in winter**

Kalanchoes are a very varied group and this one, once known as *Bryophyllum daigremontianum*, is totally different from the previous plant, as it is grown for its attractive leaves rather than the somewhat insignificant flowers. These leaves, green marbled with brown, are arrow-shaped and may be up to 10cm (4in) long. But the great curiosity is the tiny plantlets that appear within the leaf notches. When these fall off, they will take root (actually they mostly have minute roots already!) in any patch of soil they touch, giving rise to further plants; any nearby pot will soon have a kalanchoe growing beside the rightful owner! It would not be possible to have an easier plant to propagate, since it requires no effort on the part of the grower at all. The parent plant can reach a height of 60cm (24in).

Grow this novelty in any good potting mixture, and water quite freely in spring and summer.

Take care
It can become a weed! 72♦

Kalanchoe pumila
- **Full sun**
- **Temp: 5-27°C (41-81°F)**
- **Keep slightly moist in winter**

This pretty little plant is ideal for a hanging basket indoors, where it will grow and flower freely in a light window. Of course, it can also be grown in a greenhouse, where its relative hardiness will enable it to survive the lower winter temperature. The slightly thickened leaves are basically pale pinkish-green in colour, but this is almost completely masked by a grey mealy coating, giving the whole plant a delightful pearly-grey appearance. It is very free-flowering, producing masses of dark pink blooms in spring. Although these are individually only about 2cm (0.8in) across, they appear in small groups at the end of quite short stems. The plant is only about 15cm (6in) high.

To grow it in a hanging basket, line a small one with sphagnum moss or coarse peat, well damped, fill with any good potting mixture, and plant the kalanchoe in this. To propagate this succulent, cut off a few stems in spring or summer and pot them up.

Take care
Sprays can mark the leaves. 72♦

Above: **Notocactus haselbergii**
Flowers are produced on a neatly
spined white ball and the contrast
between the plant and flower colour
is most striking. This cactus does not
usually flower when young. 121♦

Above: **Notocactus leninghausii**
*This golden-spined cactus is grown
for itself rather than for the flowers,
which, although attractive, are
produced only on older, larger
plants. Nevertheless they are well
worth waiting for, and they certainly
add to the beauty of the plant.* 122♦

Above right:
Notocactus mammulosus
*This is a particularly striking
notocactus, with long, stout spines.
This free-flowering plant will set
seed quite readily. This species is
hardy even in temperate countries
and – if kept quite dry in winter – can
withstand temperatures down to
freezing. As in most freely flowering
cacti, a cold winter rest is vital.* 123♦

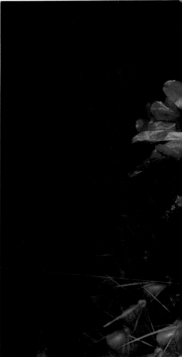

Right: **Notocactus herteri**
*The flower colour of this notocactus
makes it different from the others
illustrated here. The plant itself is
neatly rounded and has delightfully
compact spines, contrasting with its
brilliant blooms. It is reasonably
hardy and is easy to cultivate in a
well-drained potting mixture.* 122♦

Above: **Notocactus ottonis**
*This small, globular cactus clusters
freely and produces large brilliant
flowers with red centres.
Propagation by offsets is easy.* 123♦

Far left: **Opuntia basilaris**
*Most of the opuntias, or 'Prickly
Pears', do not flower as reasonably
small pot plants, but this one will
usually do so quite readily and is not
too large for a collection.* 124♦

Left: **Opuntia robusta**
*This is a natural giant, but small
specimens are attractive in a
collection. However, they are not
likely to flower.* 125♦

Above: **Opuntia microdasys**
This is the usual colour for the bunches of barbed bristles, or 'glochids', of this well-known opuntia. Large specimens may become sprawling. 124♦

Left: **Opuntia microdasys**
var. **albispina**
This variety with white glochids is particularly attractive, especially if space permits a large clump. 124♦

Below:
Opuntia microdasys var. **rufida**
A third variety, with shorter and thicker joints, and reddish-brown glochids contrasting beautifully with the dark green stems. 124♦

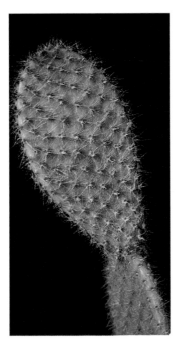

Above: **Opuntia scheeri**
As well as the typical glochids, or barbed bristles, this opuntia has a network of golden spines covering the joints. With its compact habit of growth and freely formed branches it is ideal for the average collection, and it is unlikely to become too large for many years. If and when it does, it is a simple matter to re-start by removing a few joints and treating them as cuttings. They can be potted up after a few days' drying to seal the cut surface. The best time to do this is from late spring to summer, when they should soon root. 126♦

Right: **Opuntia spegazzinii**
This is one of the cylindrical-jointed opuntias, which are less familiar than the 'Prickly Pear' shape. Its outstanding characteristic is that it can be expected to flower easily in a small pot, which is unlikely in the case of the larger-growing opuntias. The cylindrical stems tend to trail, and this cactus needs to be supported in some way, possibly on a plastic trellis as used for some houseplants. Otherwise it could be planted in a hanging basket, but be careful that it does not get tangled in anyone's hair! 126♦

Far right: Opuntia pycnantha
Do not expect flowers on this opuntia; only large old plants are likely to produce them. But the beauty of this cactus does not depend on flowers; the shape and spine colour are enough. 125▶

Right: Oreocereus celsianus
An impressive cactus by any standards, with its contrasting hair and sharp, stout spines. It is comparatively slow-growing; although it can eventually become very large, it will take years. 127▶

Below: Oroya subocculta
This may not be the easiest plant to obtain but it is worth the effort. Fortunately it is most attractive in itself, because flowers are unlikely to be produced except on large specimens. 127▶

Above: **Pachypodium lamerei**
*Long, non-succulent leaves are
formed at the top of a very succulent
stem, well equipped with stiff spines.
As the stem elongates, the lower
leaves fall and are replaced by new
ones, so that there is always a tuft at
the top. But if this succulent is
allowed to get too cold in winter it is
likely to lose all its leaves and may rot
as well. So keep it warm in winter.
Indoors it needs a sunny window and
occasional turning.* 128♦

Right: **Pachyphytum oviferum**
*An excellent example of a leaf
succulent, like sugared almonds on a
stem. The leaves are covered with a
whitish mealy coating, which makes
them very easily marked, so it is
particularly important not to finger
them or the pristine beauty of this
attractive succulent will be spoilt.
Clumps of rather unusual flowers are
produced in spring. Like many
shrubby succulents, it may become
too straggly with age, when it is
probably best to cut and restart.* 128♦

Above: **Parodia aureispina**
*This is a neat golden ball freely
producing bright yellow flowers.
Care with watering is necessary to
avoid root loss.* 145♦

Left: **Parodia microsperma**
var. **gigantea**
*Typical P. microsperma has yellow
flowers. This red variety is possibly
even more attractive.* 145♦

Right: **Parodia microsperma**
*The typically yellow flower almost
obscures the elegantly spined plant
body. Water with care.* 145♦

Above: **Pereskia aculeata**
Almost like a wild rose, this is a *strange non-succulent cactus. It* *definitely needs some support.* 146♦

Leuchtenbergia principis
- **Full sun**
- **Temp: 5-30°C (41-86°F)**
- **Keep dry in winter**

A true cactus that bears a remarkable resemblance to an agave or aloe, this strange-looking plant is the sole representative of its group. Unlike agaves or aloes, the long tubercles are part of the stem, not leaves. These tubercles can be up to 10cm (4in) long and they are tipped with groups of soft, rather papery spines. This cactus does not appear to be very free-flowering, and to give it the best chance to produce its beautiful perfumed yellow flowers, 8cm (3.2in) across, it needs as much full sunlight as possible. It is unlikely to flower as a houseplant. Propagation is said to be possible from removed tubercles, dried for a while and potted up. This is a very easy plant to raise from seed.

Water this unique cactus freely in spring and summer; the tubercles tend to spread when the plant is moist and to close in with dryness. Use three parts of a standard potting mixture added to one part of sharp sand or perlite.

Take care
Use a deep pot.

Lithops aucampiae
(Living stone)
- **Full sun**
- **Temp: 5-30°C (41-86°F)**
- **Keep dry in rest period**

These little stone-like plants are perhaps the most delightful of all the South African succulents. A large collection of them can be grown in a pan 30cm (12in) square, which makes them ideal for a small greenhouse. Lithops consist of one pair of flat-topped fleshy leaves; the stem is so short as to be invisible when the plant is potted up, and they are often described as stemless. *L. aucampiae* is one of the larger species, with leaves 2.5cm (1in) across; they are a lovely rich brown colour with darker brown dots. The golden flowers appear from between the two leaves in early autumn.

Grow this species in a mixture of half loam-based medium and half sharp sand or perlite. Keep dry all winter. Do not water until the old leaves have completely shrivelled away; this will probably be in late spring. Water on sunny days, and gradually tail off in autumn.

Take care
When watering, do not splash the leaves, as the water will leave 'chalk' marks. 74♦

113

Lithops bella
(Living stone)
- **Full sun**
- **Temp: 5-30°C (41-86°F)**
- **Keep dry in rest period**

Lithops bella has a pair of pale grey leaves with darker markings. The white flowers appear between the leaves in early autumn. This is one of the lithops that will form an attractive clump. In spring, when the old head has shrivelled away, two new heads will be found inside the old skin. The plant does not double its size every year; some years no new heads are formed, or perhaps only one head in a clump will double. Overlarge clumps can be split up. The summer growing period is the best time to do this.

No water should be given until the old leaves have completely shrivelled away, usually in late spring. Grow in a mixture of equal parts of loam-based material and grit. Do not repot annually; once every three years is sufficient. It is important to give the plant the maximum light available. The flowers open in the afternoon on sunny days, and close at night. They last for about a week.

Take care
Avoid drips from the greenhouse roof during dry rest period. 74♦

Lithops helmutii
(Living stone)
- **Full sun**
- **Temp: 5-30°C (41-86°F)**
- **Water only during summer**

Lithops helmutii has a pair of plump, apparently stemless leaves, which are bright green marked with grey and have a large 'window'. This is one of the lithops that cluster freely. Each head is about 3cm (1.2in) across. The golden-yellow flowers are also 3cm in diameter, and completely hide the leaves. The plant flowers in early autumn. The blooms open in the afternoons of sunny days and close again at night; they last for about a week.

Lithops have a definite winter resting period, when no water should be given. The new leaves grow at the expense of the old. In spring the old leaves will be partly shrivelled and the new head or heads will be seen emerging. When the old leaves are completely shrivelled away, water the plant. Water frequently until the autumn, but allow to dry out between waterings. Grow the plant in a mixture consisting of one part loam-based material and one part sharp sand or perlite. Repot every three years.

Take care
Avoid a damp atmosphere in winter.

Lithops marmorata
(Living stone)
● **Full sun**
● **Temp: 5-30°C (41-86°F)**
● **Water only during summer**

Lithops marmorata consists of a pair of almost stemless succulent leaves. The leaves are greyish-green, marbled with grey or yellowish lines. The white flower appears from the cleft between the leaves and is large enough to hide the plant body completely. The flowering period is early autumn.

An open potting mixture consisting of half loam-based potting medium and half sharp sand or perlite will ensure that the plant does not take up too much water and become overlarge. Allow it to dry out between waterings. It is essential to grow this plant in full sun, as the flowers open only when exposed to sunlight: they open in the afternoon and close at night. Lithops look their best when grown in pans surrounded by small pebbles with similar markings to themselves. It is not necessary to repot yearly. The main pests that attack lithops are mealy bug and root mealy bug. Water with insecticide.

Take care
The leaves will be marked if splashed during watering. 75♦

Lobivia backebergii
● **Full sun**
● **Temp: 5-30°C (41-86°F)**
● **Keep dry in winter**

The lobivias are a large group of cacti closely related to the genus *Echinopsis*, and many hybrids exist between them. *L. backebergii* starts by being an almost globular plant and gradually becomes more oval. It will not create much of a space problem, as it reaches a diameter of only 5cm (2in). The bright green ribbed stem will sometimes form offsets from the base. Curved dark spines spread over the ribs, about 1.5cm (0.6in) long, but may be larger if the plant is grown in strong sunlight. The beautiful flowers are carmine with a bluish sheen, and are about 4cm (1.6in) across.

This cactus is quite tolerant with regard to the potting mixture. If your standard mix looks at all compacted, add some extra sharp sand or perlite. Water it freely during spring and summer, and to encourage continued flowering add a high-potassium, tomato-type fertilizer to the water about once every two weeks during this time.

Take care
Good flowering demands a cold winter rest. 76♦

Lobivia famatimensis
- **Full sun**
- **Temp: 5-30°C (41-86°F)**
- **Keep dry in winter**

A small, particularly beautiful lobivia, this cactus is clump-forming, with individual 'heads' about 6cm (2.4in) long and 2.5cm (1in) thick. The yellowish spines on the 20 or so small ribs are so numerous and interlocking that they almost cover the stem. Flowers are normally yellow, around 5cm (2in) across, and occur in clusters at the top of the stems. Quite often they will open for several days in succession, closing at night. Don't be perturbed if your specimen produces flowers of another colour: there are varieties with orange, pink or red flowers.

This pretty lobivia is rather more moisture- and temperature-sensitive than many, so make sure that the potting mixture is very well drained by adding one part of sharp sand or perlite to three parts of a standard material. Water quite freely on sunny days during spring and summer. Stems can be removed for propagation in spring, but let them dry for a few days before potting.

Take care
Spines can hide mealy bugs. 77♦

Lobivia hertrichiana
- **Full sun**
- **Temp: 5-30°C (41-86°F)**
- **Keep dry in winter**

One of the most popular and widely grown of the lobivias, this small cactus flowers very freely, even when quite young. Stems are more or less globular, ribbed, with fairly short, bristly, spreading spines. Individual heads are about 2.5-4cm (1-1.6in) thick, and the plant rapidly forms quite a large clump. But there is no need to let it become any larger than required; heads are easily removed for propagation in spring. Merely let them dry for a few days before potting up. Brilliant scarlet flowers, produced in masses in spring and summer, may be up to 5cm (2in) across.

To get the best from this attractive cactus, let it form a reasonably large clump if space permits, preferably growing it in a pan or half-pot. Use a good standard potting mixture but make sure that it is well drained. A cold winter rest is desirable to promote good flowering, as is feeding in spring and summer.

Take care
A top dressing of gravel will protect the clump from excess water.

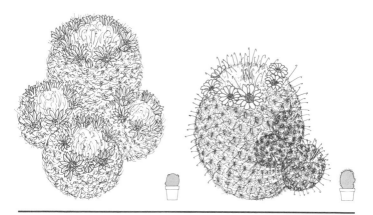

Mammillaria bocasana

- **Full sun**
- **Temp: 5-30°C (41-86°F)**
- **Keep dry in winter**

Mammillarias are the most popular of the cacti: they are small, flower freely, and have beautiful spines. *M. bocasana* is a many-headed plant that forms a cushion. The plant is blue-green and covered with silky white spines. Appearances are deceptive: underneath the soft spines are spines with hooks, which cling to the hands, clothing or anything else that touches them. The small creamy flowers form circlets around each head in spring. This is a very free-flowering plant.

This cactus needs a sunny position and ample water plus a dose of high-potassium (tomato-type) fertilizer every two weeks or so during the growing period. During winter, keep it dry. A suitable mixture is two parts of a loam-based potting medium to one part of sharp sand or perlite. Repot annually. If the plant is becoming too large, remove one of the heads, dry it for two days, and then pot it up. If the cutting is taken in spring, it will soon root.

Take care
Avoid the hooked spines. 76♦

Mammillaria bombycina

- **Full sun**
- **Temp: 5-30°C (41-86°F)**
- **Keep dry in winter**

Mammillaria bombycina is one of the beautiful white-spined mammillarias. It is a cylindrical plant that clusters from the base with age. The stems are densely clad in white spines. The reddish-purple flowers form circlets around the tops of the stems in late spring to early summer. Young plants do not flower. It seems to be characteristic of mammillarias that cream-flowered species bloom easily, even as young plants, but most of the red-flowered ones bloom only as mature plants.

An open growing medium, two parts loam- or peat-based potting mixture to one part grit, is necessary for this cactus. Since it spreads outwards, it looks well grown in a half-pot. Repot annually and examine the roots for signs of root mealy bug. Water generously during summer, but allow it to dry out before watering again. Feed every two weeks with a high-potassium fertilizer when the plant is flowering. Keep dry in winter.

Take care
Avoid a damp, cold atmosphere. 78♦

117

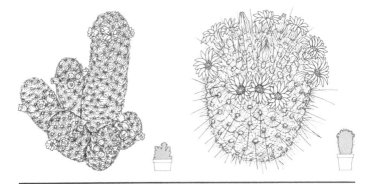

Mammillaria elongata
- **Full sun**
- **Temp: 5-30°C (41-86°F)**
- **Keep dry in winter**

Mammillaria perbella
- **Full sun**
- **Temp: 5-30°C (41-86°F)**
- **Keep dry in winter**

Mammillaria elongata is a clustering plant that consists of long finger-shaped shoots. The spines are prettily arranged in a star, and are variable in colour; plants exist with white, yellow, brown or deep red spines. The cream flowers are freely produced, even on small plants, in early spring.

This cactus needs an open mixture, two parts loam- or peat-based potting medium to one part grit. It looks at its best if grown in a half-pot. If the cluster becomes too large, remove a shoot, dry it for two or three days, and pot it up separately. The late spring is a good time to take cuttings. The plant may be watered generously during summer, but keep it dry during winter. Feed every two weeks with a high-potassium fertilizer during the flowering period. Full sunlight is necessary to maintain the rich colour of the spines.

Take care
To avoid weak spines, grow in good sunlight.

Mammillaria perbella is a silvery-white cylindrical cactus, about 6cm (2.4in) in diameter, and does not usually branch. The stem is covered in short white spines. The flowering period is early summer, when a ring of flowers appears near the top of the plant. The petals are pale pink with a darker stripe down the middle.

Grow in a mixture of one part loam- or peat-based potting medium and one part sharp sand or perlite. Repot every year and examine the roots for signs of root mealy bug. During spring and summer, water on sunny days, allowing it to dry out between waterings. During the flowering period feed every two weeks with a high-potassium fertilizer. Taper off the watering in autumn and allow the plant to remain dry in winter. Keep this cactus in the sunniest part of your greenhouse; sun stimulates bud formation and spines.

Take care
Do not allow the potting mixture to become hard and compacted.

Mammillaria spinosissima var. sanguinea

- Full sun
- Temp: 5-30°C (41-86°F)
- Keep dry in winter

Mammillaria spinosissima var. *sanguinea* has a dark green cylindrical stem and long white spines, the central spines having red tips. The purplish-red flowers are quite large for a mammillaria and form a ring in summer.

This cactus is easy to cultivate. A porous mixture consisting of two parts loam- or peat-based material to one part sharp sand or perlite is needed, and a sunny position. Repot annually. Water generously during spring and summer, but allow it to dry out between waterings. When the flower buds appear, feed every two weeks with a high-potassium (tomato) fertilizer until flowering is over. Keep it dry in late autumn and winter. When repotting, inspect the roots for any ashy deposit, which indicates the presence of root mealy bug. If found, wash the soil off the roots and replant into a clean pot; treat with a systemic insecticide.

Take care
Avoid drips from the greenhouse roof during the rest period.

Mammillaria zeilmanniana

- Full sun
- Temp: 5-30°C (41-86°F)
- Keep almost dry in winter

This is a very free-flowering mammillaria and the blooms are a beautiful reddish-violet colour; it is one of the few mammillarias of this colour to flower as a young plant. Occasionally a plant has flowers with a double row of petals, and there is also a form with white blooms. The flowering period is early summer.

The stems of this plant are cylindrical, and branch to form multi-headed clumps. Heads can be detached during summer, and used to propagate the plant. Grow in half-pots; a suitable potting mixture is two parts loam- or peat-based medium and one part grit. Water freely and feed every two weeks with a high-potassium fertilizer during spring and summer, allowing it to dry out between waterings. Let it become almost dry during winter. Keep in a sunny part of the greenhouse and inspect for mealy bug; water with insecticide.

Take care
Do not allow water to accumulate between the heads. 79♦

 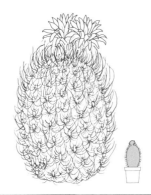

Neoporteria napina
- **Moderate light**
- **Temp: 5-30°C (41-86°F)**
- **Keep dry in winter**

Neoporterias are somewhat uncommon cacti, but they are fairly readily available nowadays and well worth growing. They have suffered in the past from the common trouble of name changing, and have been switched from one group to another. However, that need not bother those of us who merely want to grow an attractive cactus. *N. napina* is quite small, up to 8cm (3.2in) high and 2.5cm (1in) thick, although most specimens are not as large as this. The brownish-green stem is divided into many narrow ribs, arranged in a spiral and with tiny spines. Flowers are large for such a small plant, often 5cm (2in) across, and bright yellow in colour. The root is distinctly odd, something like a small turnip, and easily troubled by any excess water. Use a very well-drained potting mixture made up from one part sharp sand or perlite and two parts of a standard peat or loam material. Best to avoid full sun, and water freely on sunny days in spring and summer.

Take care
Use a deep pot for the long root.

Neoporteria nidus
- **Full sun**
- **Temp: 5-30°C (41-86°F)**
- **Keep dry in winter**

The cultivation of this little cactus is rather a challenge; it is not one of the easiest, but should not be spurned on that account, as it only needs a good, loving owner! It is a small plant consisting of a solitary, ribbed stem 5-8cm (2-3.2in) in diameter, at first more or less spherical but usually elongating with age. This stem is beautifully clothed with a mass of spines, some long and curved, others slender and almost hair-like. The reddish flowers are fairly easily produced; up to 4cm (1.6in) across.

Cultivation is not really a problem; it merely needs care. Never overwater this cactus, as damp, airless conditions at the root can cause it to disappear. If this happens in spring or summer, cut away all dark tissue, allow to dry for a week, and repot. At any other time of the year leave the repotting until the following spring. Use a particularly well-drained potting mixture made by adding one part of sharp sand or perlite to two parts of a standard mix.

Take care
Give full sun whenever possible.

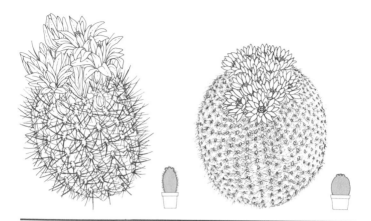

Neoporteria mammillarioides
- Full sun
- Temp: 5-30°C (41-86°F)
- Keep dry in winter

Although probably one of the less well-known neoporterias, this beautiful cactus, previously a pyrrocactus, is certainly one of the most attractive. The almost globular stem, perhaps up to a diameter of 8cm (3.2in), is bright green in colour, with many acute ribs furnished with tufts of straight, stiff spines. Although it is a neat, compact little plant, it is the flowers that make it out of the ordinary. They are of a deep rose-pink or red colour, yellowish towards the base of the petals, and are produced very freely at the top of the plant, usually several opening at one time and lasting for several days.

Grow this neoporteria in a good potting mixture. Mix one part of sharp sand or perlite with three parts of a standard peat- or loam-based material. A top dressing of gravel will help to reduce the risk of rotting off at the base, and with this protection you can water reasonably freely during spring and summer, but remember to reduce watering in the autumn.

Take care
Watch for any signs of rot. 80♦

Notocactus haselbergii
- Full sun
- Temp: 5-30°C (41-86°F)
- Water with caution

Notocacti are found growing in the grasslands of South America, and they need full sun. N. haselbergii is one of the most beautiful of these cacti. It is a silver ball: the numerous ribs are densely clad in soft white spines, which gleam in the sunshine. It does not form offsets. The flowers are carried on top of the plant in late summer; they are tomato red, an unusual colour in this group of plants. Very young plants do not flower.

N. haselbergii should not be allowed to become too wet, or it may lose its roots. A mixture consisting of one part loam-based potting medium to one part sharp sand or perlite will ensure good drainage. Water freely during summer, but allow it to dry out between waterings. Feed every two weeks with a high-potassium fertilizer during the flowering period. Keep it dry during winter. The only pests likely to be found on this plant are mealy bug and root mealy bug; water with a proprietary insecticide.

Take care
Avoid a wet, soggy potting mix. 97♦

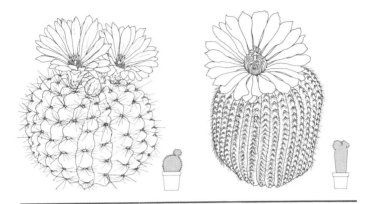

Notocactus herteri

- **Full sun**
- **Temp: 5-30°C (41-86°F)**
- **Water with care**

All the notocacti that have been in cultivation for many years have yellow flowers, but some recently discovered species have beautiful purple flowers, and one of the best of these is *N. herteri*. It is a large globular plant with reddish-brown spines. Although seedlings do not flower, the plant grows quickly and will eventually reach a diameter of at least 15cm (6in). The deep magenta flowers are formed at the top, and open in late summer.

A porous growing mixture consisting of one part loam-based material and one part sharp sand or perlite is suitable. Water freely during the summer, allowing the plant to dry out between waterings. When the buds start to form, feed every two weeks with a high-potassium fertilizer. During winter keep the plant completely dry. It is always advisable to look plants over regularly for the presence of mealy bug: treat with a proprietary insecticide if found.

Take care
Repot annually. 99♦

Notocactus leninghausii

- **Full sun**
- **Temp: 5-30°C (41-86°F)**
- **Keep dry in winter**

Notocactus leninghausii is a golden plant that branches and becomes columnar with age. The many close ribs carry soft yellow spines. It is characteristic that the growing centre of this plant tends to be on one side of the stem. The large yellow flowers appear on top of the plant in late summer. Young plants do not flower.

This cactus is not difficult to cultivate; a growing medium consisting of two parts peat-based potting mixture to one part grit, and a sunny position, will ensure a healthy plant. Repot annually. If the plant gets too large or the base of the stem becomes corky, branches may be removed in summer and used for propagation. Water freely during summer, allowing it to dry out between waterings. During flowering, feed every two weeks with a high-potassium fertilizer. Gradually taper the water off in autumn and keep the plant dry during the winter. Watch out for root mealy bug and mealy bug.

Take care
Avoid damp winter conditions. 98♦

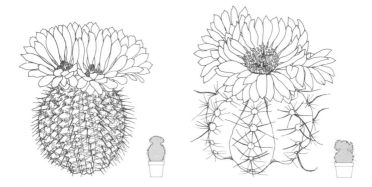

Notocactus mammulosus
- Full sun
- Temp: 5-30°C (41-86°F)
- Keep dry in winter

Notocactus mammulosus is a trouble-free plant that flowers freely while quite small. It is a globular cactus that remains solitary. The ribs carry long, stout spines, brownish in colour. The flowers, borne on top of the plant in late summer, are yellow with purplish stigmas. They are also self-fertile; the furry seed pods contain hundreds of seeds, which germinate easily if sown in the following spring.

   Grow this notocactus in a mixture of two parts loam- or peat-based material plus one part sharp sand or perlite. Repot annually. Water freely during the spring and summer growing period, but keep it dry during the winter. When flower buds form, feed every two weeks with a high-potassium fertilizer. If really dry this cactus will withstand temperatures around freezing point. Keep in full sunlight, which ensures not only good flowering but also long, stout spines. A beautifully spined plant is attractive all year.

Take care
Give a dry, cool winter rest. 99♦

Notocactus ottonis
- Full sun
- Temp: 5-30°C (41-86°F)
- Never overwater

Notocactus ottonis is quite different from other notocacti; it is much smaller, and clusters freely from the base. It is deep green, and the ribs carry slender yellowish spines. Individual heads are about 7.5cm (3in) across. The yellow flowers are about 6cm (2.4in) across.

   This notocactus is touchy about watering; to prevent it losing its roots, grow in an open mixture consisting of one part loam-based potting medium to one part grit. Grow it in a half-pot: the cluster looks better, and the roots are not surrounded by large quantities of cold, damp soil. Water freely during spring and summer, always allowing it to dry out between waterings. Feed every two weeks during the flowering period using a high-potassium (tomato) fertilizer. Keep it dry in winter. Place this plant where it will get plenty of light. The main pests are mealy bug and root mealy bug; treat with a proprietary insecticide.

Take care
Avoid damp winter conditions. 100♦

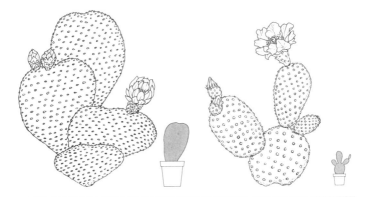

Opuntia basilaris

(Beaver-tail cactus)
- **Full sun**
- **Temp: 5-30°C (41-86°F)**
- **Keep dry in winter**

If there is any typical cactus, it must surely be the opuntia, or prickly pear, although the latter name was originally applied to the spiny fruit of a desert giant. But *O. basilaris* is not a giant and is ideal for the collection as it rarely becomes more than two segments, or pads, high, sometimes branching from the base. The pads are flattened stems (beaver-tail shape), and although almost spineless, they are dotted with clusters of dark red barbed bristles (glochids), characteristic of all opuntias, spined or not. Most opuntias do not flower readily in a collection, needing to be very large before they do so. But this one, being smaller, will often produce red blooms up to 5cm (2in) across on its second segment, when about 20cm (8in) high.

Grow this opuntia in a good porous potting mixture; extra drainage material is probably not necessary. If you winter it indoors, give just enough water to prevent shrivelling. Best kept dry if in a greenhouse.

Take care
Glochids can penetrate skin. 100♦

Opuntia microdasys

- **Full sun**
- **Temp: 10-30°C (50-86°F)**
- **Keep slightly moist in winter**

Probably the most common cactus of all, and certainly the most popular opuntia; but also the most ill-treated cactus. Witness the poor, spotted, dried-up plants so common in windows. Although it spreads over a wide area in the wild, cultivated specimens form small branched bushes, consisting of many beautiful bright green pads, or flattened stem segments, closely dotted with clumps of yellow glochids (barbed bristles) but no other spines. There are also varieties with reddish and white glochids. All are beautiful but need careful handling, because the pads are not as innocent as they look; the glochids stick into the skin at the slightest opportunity. Rarely, yellow flowers are produced.

A well-drained potting mixture is needed, and free watering in spring and summer. Give sufficient water in winter to prevent undue shrivelling and keep this cactus rather warmer than it would be in the average cool greenhouse.

Take care
Cold winter conditions cause brown spots. 102-3♦

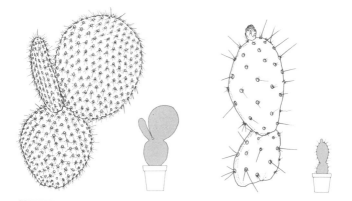

Opuntia pycnantha
- Full sun
- Temp: 5-30°C (41-86°F)
- Keep dry in winter

The fact that the name is sometimes mis-spelt as *pycnacantha* detracts in no way from the beauty of this most handsome opuntia of all, with its bright green stem and contrasting groups of reddish-brown bristly spines (glochids), in addition to the lighter-coloured, longer spines. Individual flattened stem segments or pads are about 8cm (3.2in) across, each being right-angled to the one below. Fortunately this delightful cactus does not depend upon flowers for its beauty, as they are most unlikely on cultivated specimens. Tiny cylindrical leaves appear at the ends of young pads, but soon shrivel and fall off; this is quite natural.

This species is somewhat more susceptible than many opuntias to over-wet potting mixture, which results in root loss; it is best to add about one third of sharp sand or perlite to your usual good standard material. Give water generously in spring and summer; even opuntias can wilt!

Take care
Turn indoor plants regularly.

Opuntia robusta
- Full sun
- Temp: 0-30°C (32-86°F)
- Keep dry in winter

Although this cactus is one of the giant opuntias in its native state, where it can reach a height of 5m (16ft) with bluish-green pads the size of dinner plates, it can be tamed as a pot plant and makes a good, tough specimen for the average collection. This species grows quite quickly for a cactus, and soon makes a nice plant, but without the glorious yellow flowers of desert specimens, as you will not want it to get large enough for that!

It is easy to prevent it from becoming too big: just remove one or more pads when there is any danger of this, let them dry for a few days, and start another specimen. The old plant will send out further shoots, if you want them; otherwise, throw it away! Living up to its name, *O. robusta* is hardy enough to be grown out of doors throughout the year, if it can be protected from winter rain, but it must be dry to survive. Ordinary, good potting mixture will suffice.

Take care
Protect from slugs outdoors. 101♦

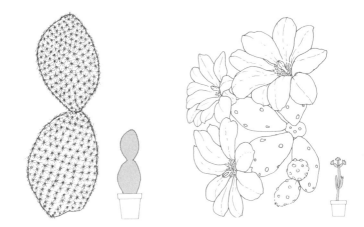

Opuntia scheeri
- **Full sun**
- **Temp: 5-30°C (41-86°F)**
- **Keep dry in winter**

By contrast with the previous opuntia, this one is ideal for the collection without any size-reducing manipulations. The flattened pads or stem segments are usually around 15cm (6in) long and 5cm (2in) broad, but older plants produce larger ones. A decorative, bushy plant results from branches off the main segment. The whole surface of each pad is covered with a network of golden spines, in addition to the inevitable barbed bristles (glochids). Flowers are yellow, but unlikely in cultivation.

Grow this cactus in a standard potting mixture, either peat- or loam-based, preferably with the addition of one third of sharp sand or perlite. Slight shrivelling of the stems may occur if the plant is quite dry in winter, as it should be if in a cool greenhouse; but in a warmer room give it just enough water to prevent this happening. You can water quite freely in spring and summer. Pads can be removed for propagation.

Take care
Mealy bugs tend to collect at the base of joints. 104♦

Opuntia spegazzinii
- **Full sun**
- **Temp: 5-30°C (41-86°F)**
- **Keep dry in winter**

There should be no trouble whatsoever in flowering this opuntia, even in a 5cm (2in) pot. It is quite different from the others mentioned: it does not have flattened 'pads' but long, slender cylindrical stems, freely branching; which in pot-grown specimens usually reach a length of about 30cm (12in) with a thickness of only 1cm (0.4in). Patches of barbed bristles (glochids) and very short spines are distributed over the stems. Large or small branches drop off at the slightest touch, usually rooting where they fall.

Grow this particularly easy opuntia in any good standard potting mixture and it should delight you every summer with its show of snow-white flowers, up to 4cm (1.6in) across, freely produced along the stems. The long, slender stems will need staking, or supporting in some way; a miniature pot plant trellis is ideal and the stems can be gently tied to this. Water freely in spring and summer; plants indoors may need a little water in winter to prevent shedding.

Take care
Handle gently. 105♦

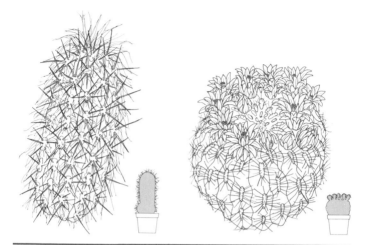

Oreocereus celsianus
- Full sun
- Temp: 5-30°C (41-86°F)
- Keep dry in winter

Although wild specimens of this cactus can reach a large size, it is relatively slow-growing, and in the collection it makes a majestic plant, probably eventually reaching a height of around 40cm (16in) and a diameter of 10cm (4in) but taking a number of years to do so from the usual small bought specimens. The cylindrical stem has a number of rounded ribs, and rows of stout, sharp, brownish spines up to 3cm (1.2in) long in larger specimens, anc appearing through a mass of silky white hairs. In cultivation this beautiful cactus does not appear to form offsets or branches, so propagation is not practicable; nor is it likely to flower. Enjoy it for itself!

Grow in a standard potting mixture; and although this is not a demanding plant, it is advisable to mix in about one third of sharp sand or perlite, to be on the safe side. Water in spring and summer whenever the potting mixture appears to be drying out.

Take care
In light potting mixtures this plant can become top-heavy. 106♦

Oroya subocculta
- Full sun
- Temp: 5-30°C (41-86°F)
- Keep dry in winter

Oroyas are somewhat problem plants among botanists, because they do not always fit into pre-conceived groups. *O. subocculta* is a very neat plant and its arrangement of ribs and spines makes it a rather unusual-looking cactus. The many blunt ribs are divided into oval segments, each with a cluster of spreading spines, also arranged in an oval pattern. These are pale brown in colour, up to 1cm (0.4in) long, thin but very sharp. The roughly globular stem will probably reach a diameter of 13cm (5in). Small specimens do not usually flower readily but when the blooms do appear they are of a beautiful orange-reddish colour, yellowish underneath. Unfortunately, they are not very large, only about 2.5cm (1in) across, and unscented.

Grow this cactus in a potting mixture consisting of one part of sharp sand or perlite added to three parts of a good standard material. Water freely in summer.

Take care
Sun will encourage flowering. 107♦

Pachyphytum oviferum

(The sugared-almond plant)
- **Full sun**
- **Temp: 5-30°C (41-86°F)**
- **Keep slightly moist in winter**

Pachyphytum oviferum forms a small shrub about 20cm (8in) high. The fat leaves, arranged in rosettes on the stems, are bluish to lavender in colour and heavily covered with white 'meal'. The white bell-shaped flowers open in spring.

This succulent is not difficult to grow. During the winter months the lower leaves will shrivel; remove dead leaves regularly, or fungus will grow on them and spread to the living plant. If the plant looks leggy ir spring, cut the rosettes off, dry them for two days, and repot. If the base of the plant is kept, new rosettes will form at the leaf scars.

Grow in a loam- or peat-based potting medium. Water freely during spring and summer. Be careful not to splash the white leaves. In the winter, give a little water to prevent excessive shrivelling of the plant. To keep a thick white coating of 'meal' grow in a strong light.

Take care
Do not finger the leaves, or they will permanently mark. 109♦

Pachypodium lamerei

- **Full sun**
- **Temp: 12-30°C (54-86°F)**
- **Keep slightly moist in winter**

On the whole pachodiums are not easy succulents and are something of a challenge, but *P. lamerei* is the least difficult and should be quite within the capability of a careful grower. The greyish succulent stem bears many thorny spines, neatly arranged in groups of three and up to 2.5cm (1in) long. Although sharp, they are not as vicious as those of many cacti. It is difficult to state an exact size, but a good cultivated specimen could be 20cm (8in) high with a thickness of about 5cm (2in). The top of the plant bears a tuft of leaves; as the stem grows they fall, to be replaced by others higher up.

Grow this pachypodium in a mix made by adding one part of sharp sand or perlite to two parts of a standard mix, and never overwater. Definitely a plant for indoors rather than the cool greenhouse in winter, but it will appreciate the extra light there in summer; indoors give maximum light and turn regularly.

Take care
Avoid cold at all times. 108♦

Above: **Pleiospilos bolusii**
Looking more like a piece of rock with a flower in the cleft, this is an extreme succulent. The flower often has a delicate perfume, somewhat almond-like. 147◆

Above: **Rebutia albiflora**
One of the smallest rebutias, this has tiny clustering heads and an all-white appearance, with white spines and unusual white flowers. 147♦

Left:
Rebutia calliantha var. **krainziana**
All rebutias are small cacti, ideal for the collection on the windowsill, if given plenty of light. 148♦

Below: **Rebutia muscula**
Another little gem, with many offsets and beautifully coloured flowers peeping out from silky white spines. Thrives in the sun. 148♦

Above: **Rebutia senilis**
Rebutias are the most floriferous of all cacti; some can almost flower themselves to death. Fortunately most produce offsets readily and are easy to propagate. This rebutia has a number of varieties with differing flower colours: pink, orange and yellow. Seed pods follow the flowers. 149▶

Above right: **Rhipsalis pilocarpa**
Rhipsalis come from tropical rain forests; they are true cacti but quite different from the more typical desert types. Many are not particularly interesting for the collector, but this one is ideal for a hanging basket. Full sunlight should be avoided in summer. 150▶

Right: **Rhipsalidopsis rosea**
This is another cactus originating from the tropical rain forests; it needs some moisture at all times, and more winter warmth than the desert cacti. Flowers are very freely produced on flattened stem segments. If you want only one cactus in a hanging basket, this is worth considering. 149▶

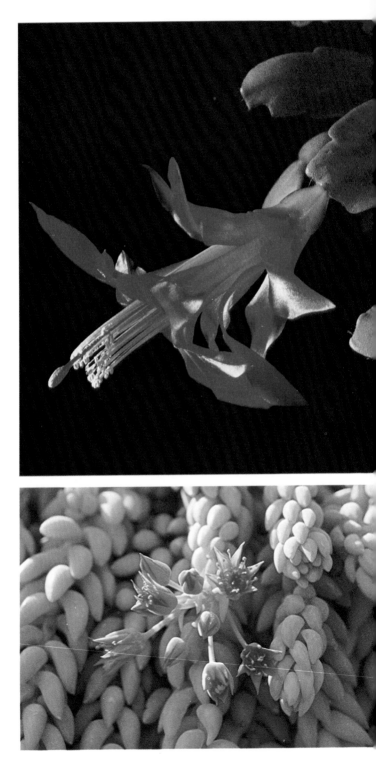

Left: Schlumbergera 'Buckleyi'
This must be the best-known cactus of all and possibly also the best-known houseplant. Whatever may be said to the contrary, it is a true cactus – one of the jungle or tropical rain forest types. Unfortunately, like many popular plants, it is not always well grown. Although watering may be reduced after flowering, this plant should never be completely dry. 150♦

Below left: Sedum morganianum
One of the attractions of succulent plants is their great variety and the so-called 'Donkey's Tail' is certainly different. With its long trailing stems, clad in small succulent leaves, it does well in a hanging basket. It is difficult to handle without damage as the leaves fall off easily. Attractive flowers are produced but usually on large plants only. 151♦

Below: Sedum hintonii
There is a vast number of sedums, including many well-known garden plants and also many rather dull species, scarcely worth growing. This, however, is a beauty, with its tiny rounded leaves clad in white glistening hairs. It is winter-flowering, which makes a pleasant change but can create difficulties with watering. Do so sparingly in winter time. 151♦

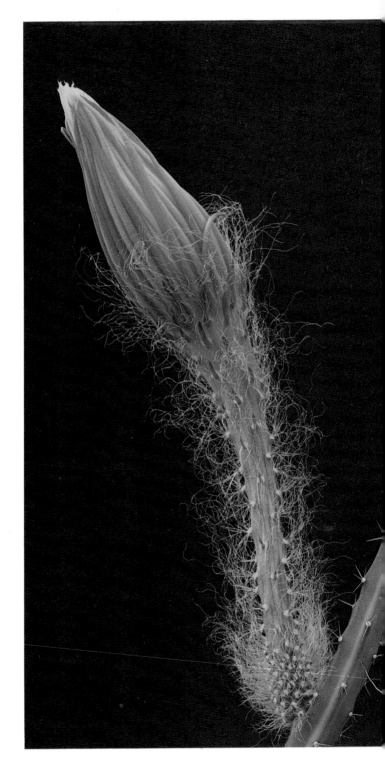

Left: Selenicereus grandiflorus
For those who have sufficient room this majestic cactus really deserves a place. The long trailing stems need some support – hardly possible in the living-room! This shows one of the immense buds, which will open during the night to a huge flower. 152♦

Right: Sedum rubrotinctum
The tiny, succulent leaves of this sedum are nicely tinted red. It is easy to propagate, as the stems tend to take root wherever they touch soil. It is usually necessary to trim the plant in order to keep it neat. This succulent is grown for its leaf colour, not its flowers. 152♦

Below: Senecio rowleyianus
Senecios show a vast difference in size; this is one of the miniature succulent ones. The photograph shows why it is known as the 'String of Beads' and also why it really has to be grown in a hanging basket. The stems take root easily on contact with the soil. 153♦

Far left: Stapelia revoluta
Stapelias are known as 'carrion flowers' because of their smell and appearance. This one has a fringe of hairs along the reflexed petals. 154♦

Left: Stapelia hirsuta
The large flowers of this stapelia are covered with fine hairs, hence the name 'hirsuta', or hairy. Stems are velvety. Sometimes flies lay eggs in the flower. 153♦

Below: Stapelia variegata
Probably the commonest stapelia in cultivation and one of the easiest to grow and flower. Also, it seems to be the one that smells worst. 154♦

Above: **Sulcorebutia totorensis**
*Sulcorebutias (not to be confused
with rebutias) are not the
commonest of cacti, and are not easy
to obtain, but they are well worth
seeking out. These delightful little
plants have strikingly coloured
flowers. This is one of the larger
sulcorebutias, but still small and
forming a cluster of compact heads.
The flowers open in succession,
which gives a prolonged flowering
period. Because of the long roots, a
deep pot is necessary; and particular
care is needed with watering.* 155♦

Left: **Trichocereus chilensis**
*All trichocerei are potentially large
cacti. They are only suitable for the
average collector because they are
slow-growing, and they make good
pot plants in their early years. Many
are somewhat dull columns, hardly
worth the space they take; but this is
one of the exceptions. It is a beautiful
plant, with stout, sharp spines of an
attractive colour. However, since
flowering is related to maturity, this
cactus must be grown for its
appearance.* 157♦

Above: **Trichocereus spachianus**
*This trichocereus will make a good
pot specimen; and if it can be given
enough space, it may well flower.
Very easy to propagate.* 157♦

Right: **Weingartia cumingii**
*A particularly free-flowering small
cactus, producing masses of blooms
in spring and summer. The spines
are quite soft.* 158♦

Below: **Weingartia lanata**
*The tufts of white wool give this
cactus its name. Very freely
produced flowers appear over a long
period. They have no perfume.* 158♦

Above: *A striking display of cacti and other succulent plants, all from the Americas. Notable among the* *specimens on show here are the beautifully varied shapes and colours of the echeveria rosettes.*

Parodia aureispina
- **Full sun**
- **Temp: 5-30°C (41-86°F)**
- **Water with great care**

Parodias are among the most beautiful of the South American cacti, but not the easiest to cultivate. They have a nasty habit of losing their roots for no apparent reason. They will regrow them but the cessation of growth can leave a scar.

Parodia aureispina is a beautiful golden ball; the spirally arranged ribs are densely covered with short yellow spines, at least one of which in each group is hooked. The large buttercup-yellow flowers are borne on top of the plant, and open during the summer. With age the plant becomes cylindrical and reaches a height of about 20cm (8in); some offsets will form.

A porous soil consisting of half loam-based potting mixture and half grit will ensure good drainage. Always allow the soil to dry out between waterings, and keep the plant dry during winter. Feed every two weeks with a high-potassium fertilizer when the buds form. Repot annually. Grow in a half-pot so that the roots are not surrounded by too much cold, wet soil.

Take care
Never overwater. 110◆

Parodia microsperma
- **Full sun**
- **Temp: 5-30°C (41-86°F)**
- **Water with care**

Parodia microsperma is globular when young, but with age it becomes elongated. It is a pale green plant with numerous spirally arranged ribs carrying many whitish spines. It will form some offsets, which may be used for propagating the plant. The golden-yellow flowers are about 5cm (2in) across and are carried on the top of the plant during the summer months.

Keep this plant in a sunny position and water it with care during the summer, allowing the soil to dry out before watering again. When buds form feed with a high-potassium fertilizer about every two weeks. Keep dry in winter. Grow in a half-pot in a mixture of one part loam-based mixture to one part grit. Repot annually. The only pests likely to attack parodias are mealy bug and root mealy bug. The odd mealy bug may be picked off with forceps but a bad infestation of either of these pests should be treated with a proprietary insecticide. A systemic one will deal more effectively with root mealy bug.

Take care
Avoid the hooked spines. 111◆

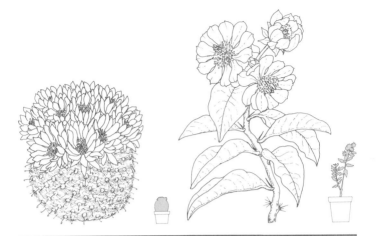

Parodia sanguiniflora
- **Full sun**
- **Temp: 5-30°C (41-86°F)**
- **Water with care**

Parodia sanguiniflora, true to its name, has large blood-red flowers. These open in summer, and make a change from the yellow flowers usual in parodias. As a young plant this cactus is globular, but it tends to become cylindrical with age. The numerous spirally arranged ribs carry many brownish spines, some of which are hooked. Some specimens form excessive numbers of offsets to the detriment of flowering. If this happens, restart the plant from an offset. For several years it will flower freely before starting to offset again.

Grow in an open potting mixture, one part loam-based medium to one part grit. Repot annually and inspect the roots for ashy deposits, which indicate root mealy bug; if found, wash off old soil and repot in a clean container. Always water parodias carefully, as they have a tendency to lose their roots if their growing medium becomes excessively wet. Feed with a high-potassium liquid fertilizer every two weeks when in flower. Keep dry during the winter.

Take care
Avoid damp conditions.

Pereskia aculeata
- **Full sun**
- **Temp: 10-30°C (50-86°F)**
- **Keep slightly moist in winter**

With this plant you will have difficulty in persuading your friends that it is a cactus at all. Pereskias are the most un-cactus-like of all cacti, but their spine formation and flower structure prove their identity. This plant is scarcely succulent at all; with its large privet-like leaves and slightly spiny long trailing stems, it somewhat resembles a wild rose. The leaves are bright green, but the variety *godseffiana* (often called *Pereskia godseffiana*) has reddish tinged leaves. The stems will need supporting in some way, with sticks or a plant trellis. In a greenhouse it can be trained up and along the roof, but the rather higher winter temperature needed makes it difficult for the cool greenhouse. Indoors, it should thrive in a light window, large enough to accommodate its stems.

Pinkish flowers, rather like those of a wild rose and about 4.5cm (1.8in) across, appear in autumn, but only on large plants. Water freely in spring and summer and feed occasionally.

Take care
Cold conditions cause leaf fall. 112▶

Pleiospilos bolusii
- **Full sun**
- **Temp: 5-30°C (41-86°F)**
- **Keep dry during rest period**

Pleiospilos bolusii is one of the stone-like plants, its speckled leaves resembling a small chunk of granite. The plant consists of one pair of very succulent leaves with flattened tops; the leaves are about 2.5cm (1in) long and almost as broad. The stem is so short that the plant is often described as 'stemless'. The heads may be split off in late summer to propagate the plant. Try to include a piece of 'stem' or leaf base.

P. bolusii flowers in autumn; the flowers open in the late afternoon to early evening, but only on sunny days. They are golden-yellow in colour and 7.5cm (3in) across.

When the previous season's leaves have completely shrivelled, the current season's leaves will be well formed. This will be late summer. Start watering at this stage and continue into the autumn, when the next season's pair of leaves will be appearing. Stop watering when they are about 1cm (0.4in) high. Grow in an open mixture, half loam-based medium and half grit.

Take care
Do not overwater. 129♦

Rebutia albiflora
- **Full sun**
- **Temp: 5-30°C (41-86°F)**
- **Water with care**

Rebutia albiflora is one of the very few rebutias with white flowers. This is a very desirable plant if space is limited; it will flower when only 1cm (0.4in) across. The flowering period is spring. The plant consists of a cluster of small heads, covered in short white spines. Individual heads can be split off and used to start new plants.

This cactus has a weak root system and should be grown in a shallow pan so that the roots are not surrounded by large quantities of cold, wet soil. A loam-based mixture or a soilless medium, to which one third sharp sand or perlite has been added, is suitable for this cactus. During spring and summer water freely, allowing it to dry out between waterings. Feed every two weeks with a tomato fertilizer when the buds appear. During the winter months keep it dry.

Mealy bug and root mealy bug are the pests most likely to attack this rebutia. A proprietary insecticide spray will deal with these.

Take care
Do not overwater. 131♦

Rebutia calliantha var. krainziana
- Full sun
- Temp: 5-30°C (41-86°F)
- Avoid overwatering

All rebutias are beautiful in the spring flowering period, but this species is outstanding. Each head is surrounded by a complete ring of orange-red flowers. The flower colour in this plant can vary from an almost true red through to a pure orange. The buds are purple.

The individual heads of this clustering cactus are cylindrical, and reach a height of about 10cm (4in). The very short white spines form a neat pattern against the green stem.

This rebutia needs a sunny position to keep it a bright colour and to ensure flowering. Any good potting mixture may be used, either loam- or peat-based. During spring and summer water freely, letting it get almost dry before watering again. When the buds form feed every two weeks with a tomato fertilizer.

Watch carefully for any signs of mealy bug, particularly around the growing point of the stems, where these woolly white pests can fade into the white wool on new growth.

Take care
Give plenty of light. 130♦

Rebutia muscula
- Full sun
- Temp: 5-30°C (41-86°F)
- Avoid overwatering

Rebutia muscula is one of the more recently discovered rebutias, and should not be confused with the less attractive *R. minuscula*. With its clear orange flowers, *R. muscula* is a beautiful addition to any cactus collection. The flowers open in late spring. The plant body is densely covered with soft white spines. It is a clustering plant and in the sun looks like a silvery cushion. The offsets may be used for propagation.

Like most cacti, *R. muscula* needs to be grown in strong light. Any loam-based mixture may be used for this plant; to improve the drainage, add one third sharp sand or perlite. During spring and summer water freely, allowing the plant to dry out between waterings. Feed with a high-potassium (tomato) fertilizer every two weeks when buds form.

Mealy bug hide between the clustering heads and suck the sap from the plant. Their white bodies blend with the plant and make discovery difficult.

Take care
Grow in a strong light. 131♦

Rebutia senilis
- **Full sun**
- **Temp: 5-30°C (41-86°F)**
- **Water with care**

Rebutias are ideal cacti for the collector without a greenhouse. They are small and will flower freely every spring if kept on a sunny windowsill. One of the prettiest is *R. senilis*: the rings of red flowers show up well against the silvery white spines. The flowers are followed by seed pods, and in autumn dozens of seedling rebutias will be found nestling around the parent plant. With age *R. senilis* clusters, forming a cushion about 30cm (12in) across. Individual heads may be removed and used for propagation.

Rebutias are not fussy about their soil, and either a loam-based or a soilless mixture may be used. In spring and summer water freely, allowing the compost to dry out between waterings. When the buds form feed every two weeks with a high-potassium fertilizer.

Carefully watch for signs of mealy bug. It is easy to miss these white pests on a white-spined plant. A systemic insecticide will be ideal.

Take care
Check for mealy bug. 132♦

Rhipsalidopsis rosea
(Easter cactus)
- **Partial shade**
- **Temp: 10-30°C (50-86°F)**
- **Keep slightly moist all year**

This is one of the jungle cacti, related to the well-known Christmas cactus, but producing its rose-pink flowers in early spring; they are about 2.5cm (1in) across. The plant itself consists of very small flattened segments, each around 2cm (0.8in) long, which, joined end to end and branching freely, eventually form a little bush. The segments carry small bushy spines along the edges and tips; they are quite harmless. Propagation is simplicity itself; just remove a small branch in spring or summer and pot it up.

Although this delightful little cactus and its many hybrids can be grown as an ordinary pot plant, it is ideal for a hanging basket. A rich growing medium is appreciated, so add about one third of peat (or leaf mould, if you can get it) to your standard potting mixture. Give a dose of high-potassium fertilizer every two weeks in spring, when buds are forming, and water freely.

Take care
Spray indoor plants occasionally with clean water. 133♦

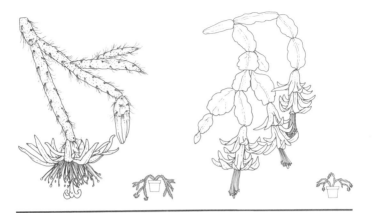

Rhipsalis pilocarpa

- **Partial shade**
- **Temp: 10-30°C (50-86°F)**
- **Keep slightly moist in winter**

At least one rhipsalis makes an interesting addition to the collection, as these are unusual cacti with an appearance quite at variance with the popular conception of a cactus. There are many species, but *R. pilocarpa* is one of the most attractive. A mass of dark green, cylindrical trailing stems, up to 40cm (16in) long and only 3-6mm (0.125-0.25in) thick, with small bushy spines make this an ideal subject for a hanging basket. White or cream flowers, about 2cm (0.8in) across, are borne on the tips of the branches; they are not very spectacular, but they do appear in winter, and they are perfumed.

Grow this rhipsalis in a good porous potting mixture, and preferably add some extra peat (sterile leaf mould is better, if available) as it needs a rich soil. Feed from time to time and water freely in spring and summer.

Take care
Best kept quite dry if wintered in a cool greenhouse. 133♦

Schlumbergera 'Buckleyi'

(Christmas cactus)
- **Partial shade**
- **Temp: 10-30°C (50-86°F)**
- **Keep slightly moist all year**

There is no doubt that this is the most popular cactus of all and the one most commonly grown, in spite of the fact that many people do not consider it to be a 'true' cactus at all, whatever that means! But it *is* a cactus, a jungle type, needing more warmth and moisture than the desert cacti. The many segments, joined end to end, are true stems (there are no leaves) and the whole plant forms a densely branched bush. Unscented flowers of an unusual shape and about 3cm (1.2in) across, are freely produced in winter at the end of segments; the typical colour is carmine but varieties exist with flowers of various shades of red, pink or even white (never blue).

Use a rich potting mixture with added peat or leaf mould, and water the plant freely when in bud and flower, feeding every two weeks at this time. Reduce the water somewhat after flowering. Propagation from segments is easy.

Take care
Buds drop if the plant is moved. 134♦

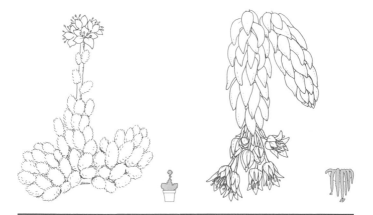

Sedum hintonii
- **Full sun**
- **Temp: 10-30°C (50-86°F)**
- **Keep almost dry in winter**

Many of the large number of sedums are somewhat uninteresting plants, but there are also some delightful little succulents, ideal for any collection. *Sedum hintonii* is one of the most beautiful of all. It consists of a mass of short stems bearing tiny egg-shaped leaves, densely covered with white hairs. Little white flowers appear in winter, always a welcome time. At flowering time the plant should be very sparingly watered, because it is very prone to rot if water becomes trapped within the leaves.

Grow this little gem in a well-drained potting mixture; add about one third of sharp sand or perlite to a good standard material, either loam- or peat-based. Although it will withstand quite low temperatures if kept dry, *S. hintonii* is better if kept rather warmer than in the average greenhouse in winter, and it makes a good houseplant.

Take care
Watch for rotting between the tightly packed stems. 135♦

Sedum morganianum
(Donkey's tail)
- **Full sun**
- **Temp: 10-30°C (50-86°F)**
- **Keep slightly moist in winter**

One glance at this unusual succulent will explain the popular name, although whether the tail-like stems resemble the tail of a donkey is a matter of opinion! Stems can be up to 90cm (36in) long, branching freely from the base, and are completely clad with small succulent leaves about 2cm (0.8in) long and 1cm (0.4in) thick. Their pale green colour is masked with a whitish bloom. The only practicable way to grow this plant is in a hanging basket. Line it with sphagnum moss and pack with a good standard potting mixture.

Any pot plants beneath the basket will soon have little sedums growing in them, as *S. morganianum* sheds its leaves easily and they take root where they fall. Very attractive rose-pink flowers are borne on the ends of shoots, but only on large mature ones. Water this unusual succulent freely in spring and summer, and never let it dry out completley or leaves will be shed.

Take care
Always handle carefully. 134♦

151

Sedum rubrotinctum
- **Full sun**
- **Temp: 5-30°C (41-86°F)**
- **Keep slightly moist in winter**

Another very attractive little sedum, this colourful succulent consists of branched stems covered with small, oval, very fleshy leaves. These are about 2cm (0.8in) long and 7mm (0.3in) thick. The basic colour is bright green but a delightful red coloration extends downwards from the tips. As the stems become longer they are likely to bend over and take root in any soil they touch. To keep a small bushy plant, remove any over-long shoots; you can always use them as cuttings. Flowers are small and yellow, but are by no means freely produced.

Any good potting mixture is satisfactory; it can be either peat- or loam-based. The plant is reasonably hardy and in winter needs only sufficient water to prevent shrivelling and leaf fall. When it is actively growing in spring and summer, you can water it quite generously, but never let the mix become soggy.

Take care
With insufficient light the red colouring is not produced. 136♦

Selenicereus grandiflorus
(Queen of the night)
- **Diffuse sunlight**
- **Temp: 7-30°C (45-86°F)**
- **Keep moist all year**

Selenicereus grandiflorus is only suitable for greenhouse cultivation; its long straggly stems are up to 5m (16ft) long and need to be trained along the roof of a greenhouse. The stems are 2.5cm (1in) thick, greyish-green in colour, and the ribs have needle-like spines.

This cactus is grown for its glorious flowers rather than the beauty of its form. The bell-shaped white flowers are about 30cm (12in) long and have a sweet scent. They open in the late evening and fade the following morning.

Grow this plant in a loam-based mixture to which bone meal has been added. Feed during the growing period with a liquid fertilizer, of the type sold for tomatoes. Repot annually. Water generously during spring and summer. Give it a little moisture during winter. When the plant becomes too large, it may be propagated by stem cuttings about 15cm (6in) long.

Take care
Protect from strong sunlight. 137♦

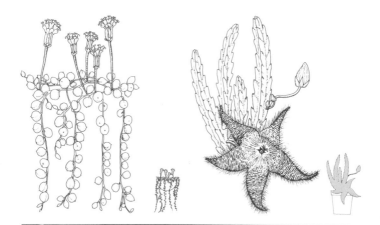

Senecio rowleyianus
(String-of-beads senecio)
- **Full sun**
- **Temp: 5-30°C (41-86°F)**
- **Keep slightly moist in winter**

Senecios are a very large group of plants; some are succulent, others are garden bushes, and they show a wide variety of shape and size. This is one of the small succulent types and a most unusual plant, with its long thin stems along which appear to be strung 'beads' in the form of spherical leaves 7mm (0.3in) in diameter. These beady stems trail and root when they make contact with the soil, so that a dense mat is eventually formed. The main interest of this little succulent is its fascinating leaf formation; the white flowers may or may not appear.

You can easily grow this senecio in a hanging basket if you persuade the stems to hang over the edge rather than rooting on the surface. To propagate, just remove a few pieces and pot them up at once. Any good potting mixture may be used; the plant is quite undemanding. Water it freely in spring and summer; feeding is not usually necessary.

Take care
Aphids can appear on the stems. 137♦

Stapelia hirsuta
(Carrion flower)
- **Full sun**
- **Temp: 10-30°C (50-86°F)**
- **Keep dry in winter**

This is a very succulent plant with four-angled velvety stems branching from the base. Although there are no spines, small teeth are borne along the angles of the stems; the stems can be up to about 20cm (8in) high and 2.5cm (1in) thick, but the plant may flower when only half this size. Of course, the most notable feature of any stapelia is its flower, with a supposed resemblance to carrion in appearance and colour. The flowers of *S. hirsuta* are up to 10cm (4in) across and of a starfish shape, the five 'arms' being purple-brown, striped with yellow; the whole is covered with purple hairs. The plant is less offensive to our noses than some other stapelias and you need not fear to keep it in the living-room.

Use a very well-drained potting mixture; add one part of sharp sand or perlite to two parts of a standard material, and top dress with gravel to prevent base rot.

Take care
Winter cold can cause black fungus spots. 139♦

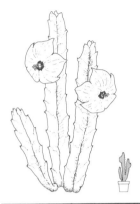

Stapelia revoluta
(Carrion flower)
- **Full sun**
- **Temp: 10-30°C (50-86°F)**
- **Keep dry in winter**

The popular name of 'Carrion flower' applies to all the large-flowered stapelias, as they are pollinated in nature by flies. This unusual succulent plant has four-angled smooth stems with soft 'teeth' along the edges. The colour is bluish-green, brown towards the growing tips. Cultivated specimens reach a length of about 20cm (8in), with a stem thickness of 2cm (0.8in). Flowers of the typical starfish shape and reddish-brown in colour have the five lobes strongly reflexed backwards (hence the name 'revoluta') making the diameter of 3cm (1.2in) much less than the opened out size. Hairs on the flowers form a fringe around the edge.

Use an open potting mixture, consisting of one part sharp sand or perlite added to two parts of a standard material. Water in spring and summer, when the soil has almost completely dried out.

Take care
Avoid base rot by a top dressing of gravel. 138♦

Stapelia (Orbea) variegata
(Carrion flower)
- **Full sun**
- **Temp: 10-30°C (50-86°F)**
- **Keep dry in winter**

This is undoubtedly the commonest stapelia in cultivation and deservedly popular for the ease with which it produces its fascinating flowers. These are 5cm (2in) or more across with blunt lobes, very starfish-like, attractively patterned with chocolate blotches on a yellow background, and with a yellow central disc.

Stems are quite small; a large specimen would be only 10cm (4in) high but freely branching.

You can easily propagate this and other stapelias by removing a stem, sometimes with roots attached, in spring or summer. *S. variegata* is one of the less demanding stapelias, but nevertheless use a well-drained potting mixture; add about one third sharp sand or perlite to a good standard material. Although this stapelia will tolerate a winter temperature below 10°C (50°F), it does better if kept rather warmer. A living-room is ideal; there is no smell in winter!

Take care
Water freely in warm weather. 138♦

Stomatium geoffreyii
- **Full sun**
- **Temp: 5-30°C (41-86°F)**
- **Keep dry during winter**

This attractive little plant will flourish either in a greenhouse or on a sunny windowsill. The many-headed plant has very short stems so that it appears to be almost 'stemless' at first glance. Each head consists of about six fleshy, triangular leaves with white 'teeth' along the edges. Each head is about 4cm (1.6in) across. The yellow flowers are produced continuously throughout the summer, opening on sunny days and closing at night.

Grow this plant in a 10cm (4in) half-pot. When the plant fills its pot, the stems will be noticeable and woody. Restart the plant by removing the heads with about 5mm (0.2in) of stem attached, and potting up in a mixture of one part loam-based medium and one part sharp sand or perlite. This is best done in early summer. Water generously during the summer, but keep completely dry during the winter.

Take care
Repot every two or three years.

Sulcorebutia totorensis
- **Full sun**
- **Temp: 5-30°C (41-86°F)**
- **Keep dry in winter**

Sulcorebutias are small, clump-forming, low-growing cacti with large tap-roots; often there is more plant below the soil than above. They are particularly outstanding for their brightly coloured and distinctive flowers. Many have very small individual heads, but this is one of the larger growing types with heads up to 6cm (2.4in) across and almost as high. By the time the plant has reached this size there will usually be a number of offsets around the base. The deep reddish-purple flowers last for about five days, but because they open in succession, the flowering period may be four weeks.

Use a deep pot to accommodate the long root. Like all sulcorebutias, this plant needs a particularly well-drained potting mixture: up to half its volume of sharp sand or perlite.

Water quite freely in spring and summer, and when it is in full bloom feed every two weeks with a high-potassium fertilizer.

Take care
Waterlogged soil can cause rot. 141♦

155

Thelocactus bicolor
- **Full sun**
- **Temp: 5-30°C (41-86°F)**
- **Keep dry in winter**

Although this is not a very large cactus in nature, it does not appear to flower readily in a collection, where the globular stem could reach a diameter of 10cm (4in). Some specimens produce offsets, but others spend solitary lives. Ribs on the stem are divided into notches, giving the effect of low tubercles, carrying the spines that give this cactus its beauty. On each tubercle there is a group of spreading spines up to 2.5cm (1in) long, and four stouter ones somewhat longer. All have the most attractive coloration, red with amber tips (whence the 'bicolor' in its name).

Thelocactus is quite an easy plant to cultivate. Use a good standard potting mixture; and add some extra sharp sand or perlite if you have any doubts about its porosity. With such beautiful spines one hardly needs flowers, but if they *do* come they are violet-red in colour. A cold winter rest will encourage them.

Take care
See that no water collects in the crown of this plant.

Titanopsis calcarea
- **Full sun**
- **Temp: 5-30°C (41-86°F)**
- **Keep dry during rest period**

'Titanopsis' means 'chalk-appearance' in Greek and describes the chalky appearance of the leaves, which closely resemble the limestone on which they grow. *T. calcarea* consists of 'stemless' rosettes 7.5cm (3in) across. Each rosette consists of two or three pairs of leaves. The grey-green leaves are wider at the tip, which is covered with whitish warts. The deep golden-yellow flowers appear during the winter months. If it is a sunny winter the buds will open during the afternoon and close again at night. In cloudy weather the buds may abort.

The growing period of this plant is winter, when it should be watered on sunny days. Keep fairly dry in summer. Grow in a half-pot in a mixture of one part loam-based medium to one part grit. The plant may be propagated by splitting the cluster. Always include a short length of stem on the heads that are removed for propagation.

Take care
Grow in the sunniest part of the greenhouse, near the glass.

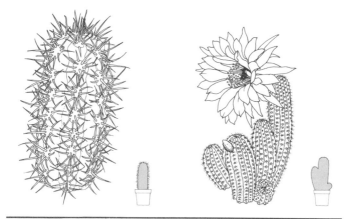

Trichocereus chilensis
- Full sun
- Temp: 5-30°C (41-86°F)
- Keep dry in winter

Trichocerei are pretty when small, but this cactus will not grow too large during the lifetime of its owner. This one is sometimes offered for sale and is well worth acquiring. With naturally large-growing cacti it is difficult to state a definite size but a good cultivated specimen would be about 20cm (8in) high and 5-8cm (2-3.2in) across after many years. But you are likely to buy this one at around 5cm (2in) high. The long golden-brown, stout spines arranged along the many-ribbed bright green stems make this a most attractive cactus, which is just as well, because it is of no use to expect flowers except on very large specimens. But the white flowers, when produced, are beautiful and pleasantly perfumed. Because the stem is unbranched, propagation from cuttings is not possible.

Any good standard peat- or loam-based potting mixture will do for this very tolerant cactus and you can water it freely in spring and summer.

Take care
The spines are needle-sharp! 140♦

Trichocereus spachianus
- Full sun
- Temp: 5-30°C (41-86°F)
- Keep dry in winter

This trichocereus is another naturally large cactus that makes a good smaller specimen for a collection. It could easily reach a height of 30cm (12in), with bright green stems eventually branching from the base. The blunt ribs bear only quite short spines, and the plant is reasonably easy to handle. If allowed to become large enough it may well respond by producing large greenish-white flowers from the top, opening at night. But the main use for this plant is as a grafting stock for other cacti, and unless you want a large specimen, it is simplicity itself to produce many small ones. If any branch is cut off, not only will it root if given the usual few days' drying-off period, but the stump will send out a ring of offsets, which can be removed and potted up in their turn.

With a good standard porous potting mixture, peat- or loam-based, it is not necessary to add extra drainage material. Water freely in spring and summer.

Take care
Tall plants become top-heavy. 142♦

Weingartia cumingii
- **Full sun**
- **Temp: 5-30°C (41-86°F)**
- **Keep dry in winter**

This free-flowering small cactus is sometimes included with *Gymnocalycium*, because of also having hairless flower buds. But, apart from this, the resemblance is not very great. *W. cumingii* is a bright green, spherical plant with a maximum diameter of about 10cm (4in), and divided into a number of spiral, notched ribs. The golden spines are usually less than 1cm (0.4in) long and quite soft and bristly. Deep yellow flowers are freely produced around the top of the stem in spring and summer, about 3cm (1.2in) across.

If you keep this plant indoors, be sure to put it in the coldest room in winter (but with good light) in order to encourage flowering the following year. In a greenhouse there should be no problem. Grow this weingartia in a mixture of a good standard material and sharp sand or perlite in the proportion of three to one. Water freely in spring and summer, and give a feed every two weeks with a high-potassium fertilizer.

Take care
Watch for mealy bugs at the base of the flowers. 142♦

Weingartia lanata
- **Full sun**
- **Temp: 5-30°C (41-86°F)**
- **Keep dry in winter**

The 'lanata' in the name of this delightful cactus is derived from the clumps of white wool scattered over the stem, which is roughly spherical and reaches a diameter of about 10cm (4in). The spiral ribs are deeply notched so that the appearance is of a mass of large tubercles rather than ribs. It is on the ends of these tubercles that the woolly hair appears, more towards the top of the plant, and also clumps of stiff but not very stout pale brown spines, about 2cm (0.8in) long. For sheer beauty the golden yellow flowers are unsurpassed. Although only about 3cm (1.2in) across, they are produced in profusion around the top of the stem, and in a good year spring or summer flowering is often followed by one in the autumn. The flowers last for several days, but unfortunately they are scentless.

This is not a demanding cactus, but to be on the safe side add about one third of extra sharp sand or perlite to a good standard mixture. Feed during the flowering period with a high-potassium fertilizer.

Take care
Water freely spring and summer. 143♦

Index of Common Names

Picture Credits

PRINTED IN BELGIUM BY

INTERNATIONAL BOOK PRODUCTION